The **Mourning's Light:**
Life after Child Loss

Patricia Sheveland

Patricia Sheveland
Positive Aspects Today, LLC

This book is an original publication of Positive Aspects Today LLC
www.patsheveland.com

Library of Congress Control Number: 2016939142

Sheveland, Patricia

The Mourning's Light: Life after Child Loss/Patricia Sheveland
Printed in the United States of America

Paperback ISBN: 978-0-9973839-0-4
E-book ISBN: 978-0-9973839-1-1

Cover design: LilyTiger Creative, LLC
Cover Image: iStockphoto.com
Interior design: Taylor Zappa

This book is in memory of all the children who have transitioned to a new life after death, and in honor of all of their families who grieve them, especially my parents:

Ruth and Harold Huss.

Jesus said, "Let the little children come to me, and do not hinder them, for the kingdom of Heaven belongs to such as these."
(Matthew 19:14)

New International Version (NIV)

CONTENTS

INTRODUCTION

This book was started in December 2014, but the *real* story began sixty-three years ago...

The night my brother died...

The concept for this book began when I volunteered at a grief camp for kids, unknowingly entering into a stream of synchronicities leading to what would be a catalyst for me... a catalyst to help me gain an understanding that my mom has been and continues to be a grieving mother.

My goal in writing this book was to help my

mom find some healing from her grief by being able to talk about my brother and how his death impacted her. To allow her to give voice to the grief she has held tightly to her breast for so many years.

Little did I know at the time, that this book would also become a tool of healing for me (as the child of a grieving family), and a way for other grieving families to tell their stories of grief and loss. For many, this book became the forum to finally be heard after years of silence.

This book has also helped me understand why I was destined at a very early age to become a *Mourning's Light,* by providing love, hope, and support to those who grieve... helping them to find purpose and joy in their lives after the death of their child.

I believe God sent a soul to earth the day I was born... a little soul reborn into a grieving family through a little girl... a little girl with a healing spirit... a little girl destined to be the voice for not only this little soul, but the souls of many...

The little soul who came forth the day I was

born was...

Gregory John Huss

My Brother... My Spirit... My Life...

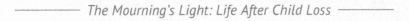

Gregory John Huss

June 21, 1952 – October 12, 1952

(Artist: Taylor Zappa)

Part I

Struck by Lightning

Chapter 1

The First Epiphany

Have you ever had an "epiphany"... a time when you found yourself having a profound insight, which almost causes a physical reaction within you? I had that type of experience in 2012 when I was sitting on a plane...

I was flying home from a work trip and began reading the book ***Heaven is for Real***, written by Lynn Vincent and Todd Burpo.

A co-worker had told me about this book because we had been talking about life after death one day at work. I think the conversation started because I was telling her how my mom and I were talking about my brother, Greg, who had died years ago, and the fact that my mom was still engulfed in some pretty deep emotions of grief. Greg would have been sixty years old on his birthday in 2012, which is the trigger that got my mom to start talking about him.

I downloaded *Heaven is for Real* on my e-reader and for some reason (which I have later come to know as *synchronicity*), I was reading *that particular* book on *that particular day* on the plane. Normally I do not read books for pleasure when I am flying on work trips but on this flight, I opened up the book and started to read...

Heaven is for Real is the story of a three-year-old named Colton Burpo, a little kid who had a *near-death* experience while he was in surgery for a ruptured appendix. He was one sick little boy with one hot little appendix when he arrived at the hospital and was taken into surgery.

Colton would make a comment here and there to his dad about seeing family members who had died when he was in Heaven... information that he really had no way of knowing, for instance, family members that he had never met before they died.

He also talked about spending time with Jesus and he had a very particular picture of Jesus in his mind... not the typical pictures of Christ that are more commonly portrayed in paintings and religious references. As Colton shared more and more of his time in

"Heaven", his dad decided to write Colton's story.

I know some people will think that the story is made up; that because Colton's dad was a minister, Colton's recollections were stories that he heard and imagined while under anesthesia. Others may feel that way, but this book has had a profound impact on me personally, and the book's impact has been felt by many other people I have shared it with.

If it had not been for reading that book on the plane, I am not sure if my story would have ever been written or understood...

On that flight, I was partway through the book when I closed the cover to my *Nook* and looked out of the airplane window... and then **IT** happened... I had **THAT MOMENT**... that surreal moment when my body felt like an electrical shock moved through it.

The realization hit me so hard that it almost felt like a voice erupted within me and told me this **Truth...** the **Truth** that my brother Greg's soul had been reborn through my birth, when I came into this world six years after his death.

I know what you are probably thinking... *oh yeah sure, it is going to be one of those books where someone is making up some story for sensationalism... I mean, who really believes that the soul of someone who died can be reborn through someone else?*

I have to tell you that I was so overwhelmed with this thought that a tidal wave of emotion took hold of my body and my heart. I literally just sat there stunned... *where the heck did all this come from? Why am I having such a defining moment at this time? Am I going crazy?* I was so overwrought with emotion, yet absolutely certain that Greg was there with me in my body and in my soul...

It is important for you to understand that I have always had a strong sense of spirituality, but I was definitely **not** a *Bible thumping, dyed in the wool* follower of any specific religion. I was raised Catholic but at a very young age, I questioned some of the rules of the Church. I never understood the whole idea of Purgatory and I questioned in my mind, *if God was an all-loving, all-forgiving God... where did "Hell" come into the picture?*

Some things just didn't make sense to me even at a very young age. To this day, I do not believe in a *Hell* where the dead have to spend their eternal lives in a burning pit. I believe

Hell is a metaphor used in various religions... the "hell" we experience on this earth like trauma, disease, abuse, addictions, and most certainly death of our loved ones, are the kinds of things that I believe make up the flames of hell on Earth.

Having this dramatic experience on the plane was beyond my comprehension... I was shaking and near tears as I waited for the plane to land. I could not shake off the feeling of that electrical "shock" that felt like it entered through the top of my head and surged throughout my body, finally resting in my heart... and into the depths of my soul...

When I landed at my destination, my daughter met me at the baggage claim area, and all I could do was look at her and say, *"I just had the strangest experience in my life!"* We sat down in a couple of chairs waiting for my luggage to come down the baggage chute when I started blabbering on about what had just happened to me on the plane.

Thankfully it was Brittany who had met me that day because she has this huge, loving heart that never judges... she just listens. I am sure that day was a bit weird for her as this woman who she has known for most of her life... a woman with great strength and fortitude was now sitting in the airport baggage claim area, eyes filled with tears and a shaky voice, as the story just poured out...

When things happen for "no reason", there most likely is a reason. Take time to reflect on what you learned during that moment and see where your mind takes you...

Chapter 2

Is Heaven For Real?

As I said earlier, I cannot tell you with absolute certainty that everything Colton Burpo said or experienced is fact. I have never met Colton or his parents, so to sit here and tell you it is truth word for word would not be appropriate for me. However, this book made a huge difference not only in my life but also in the lives of several others...

After I read the book, I bought a paperback copy for my mother. I wanted her to read it and hopefully gain some comfort in knowing that she will be reunited with Greg again when she transitions from this earthly life.

When my mom told me that she had finished reading the book, her voice was the most animated I have heard it to be in my life... literally. She said, "I always wondered if I would ever see Greg again, and now I know that I will!"

She then told me that she loaned it to her sister, my Aunt Bev, but she told her sister that she had to give it back. This was a big deal because my mom would give her sister anything without ever thinking about getting it returned, so I knew the book had a profound impact on my mother.

In December of 2012, my mom, my brother Steve, and I took a good friend of Mom's out for dinner. My mom's friend, Dorothy, had a child who died unexpectedly when he was twelve years old. During dinner, I asked some questions about her son, Scotty, and she told us about his death. Interestingly, this was around the time of his birthday.

I have found that our loved ones do make appearances to us during important dates and times from their physical lives. For instance, my dad passed away over twenty-five years ago and I may not think about him for long periods of time and then he pops into my mind. When he pops into my head unexpectedly, I make sure I check my calendar because he usually *shows up* around the time he died or around his birthday.

After we arrived home from dinner that night with Dorothy, my mom said to me, "I want to give Dorothy that book, _Heaven is for Real_". I felt an urge to go and get the book that night, driving twenty miles to the closest Walmart in the dead of winter.

I felt compelled to get the book because there was a voice in me saying "get the book to Dorothy right away..." So my husband and I took off and drove to Brainerd at 10:00 pm to hit that Walmart, where I picked up a couple more books because intuitively, I knew that I should have some extra copies on hand.

I drove over to Dorothy's home the next day and gave her the book, in which I had written a little note from my mom and I. I told her that we hoped it would give her some comfort in knowing that Scotty is in the most beautiful place imaginable and that someday she would be reunited with him.

Dorothy was so appreciative that we had thought of her, and within a couple of weeks, she called my mom, thanking her profusely for the book. She had read it and had even discussed it with her pastor at her church. He had never heard of the book, so she loaned it to him so he too could read the words of this inspirational book.

Ten months later, Dorothy died from cancer.

It was then that I knew why I had been given the message to get the book to her right away. That book was more than a gift to console her about Scotty; it was also a gift of *Peace. Peace* in assuring her that she would be reunited with her child and her husband in Heaven when she died.

Never did we (my mom and I) imagine that Dorothy would die less than a year later. I am so happy that I listened to the *nudging* inner voice to run to Walmart that late December evening!

Sharing this book was a message that I was told to follow through on by my *inner voice*, a voice I now believe is the voice of Divinity that has always resided within me.

You can call the voice my *Angels*, my *Spiritual Guides*, *God*, or my *Higher Self* - it really doesn't matter - I just know there is a voice within me which I listen to with much more intent now than ever before.

I also gave a copy of the book to my friend, Julie, around the same time that Dorothy received her copy. Julie loves to read, and I thought she might like the story. After Julie read the book, she gave it to her mother,

Elaine, who in turn, then loaned it to another women in her townhome complex.

Elaine had lost a baby when Julie was a little girl, and after reading the book, she was so moved by the story, she felt compelled to share it with others.

As you will read later on in the book, Julie's mother, Elaine, has her own story to tell, and this book gave her the forum to tell that story to know she,too, has finally been *heard*.

As you can see, the story *Heaven is For Real*, began as a thread that started to weave into the tapestry of my story and soon, more threads were added through the stories of other families who have experienced sorrow after the death of a child.

Chapter 3

The Second Epiphany

When my Godmother died in late December of 2012, I was looking on-line at the local mortuary's web site for the visitation and funeral service times. I notice a small logo on the bottom of the website. The logo was a red heart with a blue balloon attached to it with the words *Children's Grief Connection* written next to it.

I was intrigued by the logo and for some reason; I had to look up this organization on the Internet to figure out what it was all about. I learned through the web site that *Children's Grief Connection* provides camps for children and their families when someone close to the child has died. I knew *immediately* that I had to fill out my application and volunteer at the camp.

Again, here I am asking myself, "*Why? Why am I feeling the need to volunteer at a kids' camp?*" I am not a particularly maternal or nurturing type of person, so volunteering for a kids' grief camp was not something I would ever think of doing, yet there was some invisible driving force pushing me to be a part of this organization, to help kids who were grieving.

I got all my paperwork in order, including getting references from a couple people from work as well as obtaining a background check, to make sure I was an okay person to work with kids.

I went to my first camp in April of 2013, nervous and thinking *"What the heck am I doing here over a hundred miles away from home, at a camp, with not one single person I know?"* I could not believe that I had just jumped in and decided to do this volunteer thing; it really was not part of my normal persona.

I was asked to take on the duties as the "camp nurse." The woman who was my mentor and roommate was a veteran volunteer who had worked close to thirty camps, many of those as camp nurse. She told me that I would become "addicted" and want to volunteer at all the camps. Yep, she was spot on.

I was addicted before the weekend was over! That first camp changed something deep inside of me, and I knew that I was going to be an advocate for these kids, their families, and this camp. I came back in November 2013 as camp nurse in the kids' program once more. I was named *"Nurse Pat with the purple hat"* by one of the other volunteers!

In the spring of 2014, I was asked to work in the family program, which is the camp where the adult family members go while the kids are at the *Hearts of Hope* kids' program.

The purpose of having separate camps was designed because kids and adults grieve very differently. A child's view of death is different depending on the stage of development (age) of the child. Younger children are very concrete thinkers and for them to grasp the concept of death takes a very different view versus a teenager or an adult.

I learned how important it is for both the parents and the children to have their own space to grieve apart from one another. I also learned the concept of adults having *layered grief* - they not only grieve for the loss of their loved one, but they are saddened to watch their children grieve.

My first time at the adult camp was significant for me because my son's father had died a few months prior. Watching my child grieve was probably the toughest time for me in my life to date. Not being able to "fix" things for my son and not being able to stop him from hurting was horrible. I wanted to take away his pain and I couldn't. I was helpless. As I sat through my first family camp, I could totally relate to the other parents when they talked about how hard it was to watch their children grieve.

It was at the next camp in November 2014, when my second *epiphany* struck me - another lightning bolt shocked my system. I have definitely learned through this journey that one can be hit by spiritual lightning a lot more frequently than being physically struck by a bolt from the sky!

During this particular camp, I spent time listening to and feeling the emotions arising from two couples and a young single mom, all who were grieving the death of their children.

I watched two of the mothers as they talked, as they cried, as they got angry, as they felt guilty, and then as they cried some more. The rollercoaster of emotions climbed to a peak and then plummeted back down. The emotional ride took sharp turns as their grief would leave them literally gasping for air.

I also watched the two fathers who had difficulty expressing how they felt. They were very uncomfortable, squirming in their chairs and looking down at their hands. I had a sense that they felt like they just wanted to disappear - to vanish into thin air. Their sadness was palpable. Their anger was livid. Their guilt was gut wrenching.

As I drove home that Sunday afternoon after camp, the insight of my second epiphany hit me without warning, and the tears started flowing. The rivers of tears were streaming down my face, blinding my eyes as I was driving down the freeway.

I realized that I was one of those kids at camp... I was the child of one of those

parents whose grief went well beyond "heart wrenching." I was the child whose sibling had died.

The only difference between the children at camp and me was that I was 56 years old and my brother had died over 60 years ago...

Synchronicity: When events happen that appear to be coincidence but seem to have greater meaning.
Allow yourself to think beyond practicality and move into other possibilities such as coincidences being proof of Spiritual Interactions within your life.
As you open your mind, more of these incredible events will continue to come forth.

Chapter 4

A Curious Little Girl

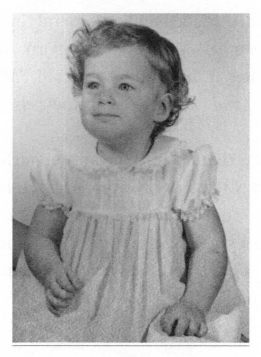

I was born on June 22, 1958, coming into this world as the fourth child of Harold and Ruth Huss, or so I thought. It wasn't until a few years later that I would learn that I was not the fourth child in the union but was actually number five.

I do not know what life for my parents was like at the time of my birth, however one of my parents' friends told me several times that she remembers the day I was born. My dad greeted her at the hospital and said, *"My life is complete, and I do not need anything else"*.

To know that my birth meant so much to my dad brings tears to my eyes, because *I get it*. When my son was born, I too felt that nothing more was needed in my life, and I had been given the greatest gift known to mankind - the gift of new life.

As you will see later in this book, I believe my Dad knew that Greg's spirit had come back into his life when I was born. I believe that Dad felt his life was "complete" because he not only gained a daughter, but his baby boy, who died six years before, had come back into his life.

As a little girl growing up, I was very curious, always interested in listening to the stories told when my extended family would get together. I was also interested in looking at old photos of my family and ancestors. I felt a *need* to know the family I was a part of, and most of all, to understand what my parents were like when they were young - *who did they hang around with? What was their life like all those years ago?*

My mom kept old photo albums up in one of the attics of our two-story home. As a little kid, I would climb the steps to the upper level and walk into the attic at the top of the stairs, digging through the old cedar chest and other memorabilia that was stored up there.

I would pull out the old photo albums and scrapbooks, sit myself down cross-legged on the floor and become engrossed in looking at people I had never met and seeing my family when my brothers were young and I was not yet born. There seemed to be so much mystery in not having been a part of that earlier time.

I spent many hours up in that attic, looking at the pictures of people I had never known. I remember being particularly drawn to a couple of pictures of my Great Grandmother McCaffery (my dad's grandmother). I would softly move my fingers across the photos of her and all of the young children surrounding her, sensing a connection with these people. I learned that my twin cousins were in the picture with their brother, Bobby, who had died as a young kid.

This elderly woman and the cousin who died years before I was born, intrigued me. To this day, when I look at those old photos, I am still drawn to those who died prior to my birth.

I feel like I have always had a connection with them in some way, even though I had never met them in this physical world. I feel a sense of closeness to my Great-Grandmother McCaffrey, as if I had been one of those young children surrounding her in the old photos.

I wonder if this "relationship" I have with those who died prior to my birth is due to my belief that Greg's spirit returned to this physical world on the day I was born? Could my feeling of connection with those who had died long before I came into this world be because a part of my soul had connected with them from another dimension before I was born?

I have no memories of going over the photos with my mom, but I must have asked her tons of questions about the people in the pictures, since I have always known the names of the people, their relationships with my mom or dad, and whether they were relatives of ours. I somehow gathered a lot of information at a very young age about the people in my parents' lives from those times I spent in that attic.

Now it is time to turn back the clock of time and introduce you to two of the most influential people in my life, my parents

Harold Huss and Ruth Schmitt. It is with them where our story really begins.

Chapter 5

The Book of Ruth

My mom was born on July 5, 1924, the first of two children born to Alois and Anna Schmitt. My Grandpa Schmitt, "Al", had been a bachelor farmer until he married my grandmother. I assume he was in his late twenties or possibly early thirties when they married. My grandmother was nine or ten years younger than him, and she was in her early twenties at the time of their marriage.

My grandfather was a farmer through and through; he loved working the land and caring for his cattle. It was the perfect life for this soft-spoken man. He was a man who had endured great hardship living through the Great Depression, and surviving the horrors of the battlefields in WWI.

My grandmother was born in Evanston, Illinois, the eldest of six girls. She was a city girl and not formally educated. She may have lived life in the city, but she definitely did not come from a wealthy family.

When she went to work as a young woman, she would bring home her pay and give it to her father to help support the family. One of her jobs was playing the piano at a silent movie theater. Imagine a young girl poised on a piano bench playing music to the scenes on the silent screen - pretty cool to think about!

When Grandma was in her eighties, she asked me to go to Kmart and buy her one of those large electronic keyboards. She sat it on her lap or on a small table in front of her and would tentatively finger the keys, pulling memories from long ago as she would softly re-create the music of her past.

I am not sure how my grandparents met or how the decision to get married occurred because they were vastly different in both upbringing and personalities. Grandpa was a very quiet man, while Grandma was the total opposite, an outspoken woman with a very definite point of view. They were "second cousins" (their grandfathers were brothers), so I assume that they met through some extended family gatherings.

My grandfather, the farmer from Minnesota, tried to live in the big city of Evanston, Illinois, but his heart was not into it.

I recall reading an old article from the society section of the local newspaper where it mentioned that my grandfather had travelled to Minnesota with his six-month old daughter, Ruth (my mom), and had an extended stay in Minnesota.

Imagine a thirty-something bachelor farmer, now married and father to a baby girl, taking full responsibility for the care of his daughter in another state, while his wife stayed in the city with her family. I find it a bit strange that my grandmother did not travel with them, and even stranger that she would allow her baby daughter to be away from her for so many months.

My grandmother was known to be a bit of a *drama queen* in her day, and it has been told that when she did not want to do something, she was stubborn as a mule. It probably was very difficult for my grandmother to contemplate a life far away from her birth home and her family. Add in moving onto a farm, away from the big city of the Chicago area must have created some very real turmoil within her heart.

My grandparents had another daughter, my Aunt Bev, who was four years younger than my mom. They were all living in Minnesota by that time, in a home that housed my mother, Aunt Bev, my grandparents, great-grandparents, and my great-great-grandmother, Julianna.

There also was a young woman who was somehow related to the family living with them. I think she may have been orphaned, and my mom tells me that she died at a fairly young age, a teenager. Back in that time, the wake was held in the family's home and my mom vaguely remembers this young girl "laid out" in the living room prior to her funeral and burial.

It is hard to imagine all of these people housed in a small dwelling that used to be a chicken coop. Today we have huge houses on small lots, but back in the 1920's and 30's, the farmhouses were small structures on large pieces of land because the land was a farmer's livelihood.

My grandparents worked extremely hard on the farm, milking cows, raising chickens for egg laying and butchering, and growing vegetables and fruits for their meals. Grandpa would never let his girls work in the barn or in the fields.

He was extremely protective of his two girls and knew that farming could be a very dangerous line of work. With cows and bulls that were unpredictable in their behaviors, and a tractor that was massive in size, it was a dangerous environment for two little girls.

My grandmother was not a very maternal woman. She had the typical stoic German personality, where hugs and expressions of love were not freely given out. I share this because I feel it is important to understand my grand-mother's personality, which I believe played a significant role in what my mother experienced after the death of my brother.

By the time my mom became of the age to go to school, her grandparents had moved from the farm and into town. Living in town meant she was five miles away from the farm; five *long* miles of dirt roads to travel.

Today, five miles is nothing to travel, taking us only ten minutes or so depending on the speed limit. In the 1930's, travelling into town across dirt roads by car could take thirty minutes or more. It was a real jaunt to "go to town."

My grandparents wanted to give their daughters a good education, so at the age of six, my mother moved into town to live with her grandparents so she could attend the Catholic grade school. From that time forward, my mom viewed her grandmother as the *mother* figure in her life, seeing her as more of the maternal person in her life, than her own mother.

When my mom was fourteen, she was sent to the city of Mankato (which was forty-five miles away) to attend the Catholic boarding school run by the School Sisters of Notre Dame. Living away from home with limited visits with her own family created a situation where the nuns running the boarding school influenced her teenage years more than her family or peers.

Mom lived a very "cloistered" life, as one

would expect living with the nuns and other young Catholic girls. She still talks to this day about "having never learned to be a good wife or mother" because she was raised in a boarding school during those informative and impressionable years from the age of fourteen until her high school graduation.

Passing the time as a child in that attic, I loved looking at pictures of my mother during those high school days and her early adulthood. She was exquisitely beautiful with her dark wavy hair and a very fashionable style.

She also had such a look of innocence in her face and always appeared a bit shy in front of the camera. Looking at the old photos of her, I see a very gentle soul lurking behind those beautiful eyes. I would often wonder what she was like in her youth: *What was her life like* and *who really was the person in those pictures?*

Isn't it funny that I was curious about my own mother when I lived with her on a daily basis? One would think that I would have known who she was, her personality, and the things that she enjoyed in life. But I didn't.

I had always felt a bit of mystery surrounding my mother. She was a quiet woman and very formal in her manners. She always referred to herself as *Mother* when talking about herself, never using the more informal term of *Mom*.

To this day, if she is calling one of us kids on the phone, she will say, "Pat (or Stephen, David, Michael)? This is your mother." She calls my brothers by their full proper names...

very reserved, even after ninety-one years on this earth.

Looking through her scrapbook and old photographs back in my *attic days* created an even deeper sense of wanting to know more about her. My curiosity must have led the way for me to ask lots of questions about the people in the photographs and her life as a young woman.

I found out through pictures that my mom played on a basketball team at her all girls' Catholic boarding school in Mankato. Imagine a petite, 4'11" shy, young girl being on the basketball team! My mom was never the athletic type (except for golf and bowling), so picturing her dribbling a basketball down the court is really humorous to me; a very different picture than the woman I know as my mom.

I learned from the scrapbook that my mother was a writer, a passion not only I, but also my son Trevor, inherited from her. She was so eloquent in her descriptive prose, taking great care in her writing and use of words - very similar to how she lived her life - with great precision and care.

The scrapbook also allowed me to see parts of my mom's life that were hidden deep...

It was an eight by ten photo of a young man that gave me an introduction to "Ben." Ben was the young man my mother was engaged to before she met my Dad.

Being a curious child, I must have inquired about this guy when I saw his picture, and Mom apparently told me that she had been engaged to him. I didn't make much of it as a little girl but as I was writing this book, I came to understand who this man was, and the impact his relationship had on my mother, at a much deeper level.

Recently, I spent some time asking mom how she met Ben. She shared this part of her story: She met him on a streetcar "*in the city (St. Paul).*" *Hmm,* I wondered, *could this have been the real streetcar named Desire?*

I can picture her in my mind's eye, on a streetcar, dressed in the style of the forties. I see her clothed in a neatly pressed dress, nylons and classic pumps. She probably had been wearing a hat over her dark, long hair and perhaps she was wearing gloves – a well put-together young woman with a shy smile.

When they met on that streetcar, she said they started talking with each other and realized they were from the same small town south of the Minnesota River. It was apparent from the way she told her story that my mom was quite enamored with this guy, and over time, a marriage proposal and formal engagement followed.

Ben was in the Navy, and my mom said that the last time he had spoken to her was when he had called and asked her to meet him in Florida to get married. She thought it was a strange conversation and I am still not clear how they ended that call, but that was it. She never heard from him again.

One minute this beautiful young girl was engaged and planning to get married, and then all communication ceased with no explanation.

Ben returned to their hometown and I asked mom if she had ever seen or talked to him after he came home. She said that after seeing him in church a few times, where he would never acknowledge her, she decided one day to follow him out of church. She told him, "We need to talk."

She said she told him, "This apparently isn't going to work out," and gave him back her engagement ring. He never said a word, only taking the ring she handed to him, and they walked away from each other, the final ending of the relationship.

Mom found out later from friends that he had some type of a mental breakdown while he was in the service and he had never fully recovered. He lived with his mother until she died, and then lived with an aunt of his for the remainder of his life. He never married... and died many years ago.

Mom told me that someone who knew his family well, told her years later that it was a blessing that they had never gotten married. Ben was apparently a very troubled young man, and it sounds like my mother would have been destined to a very difficult life if she had gotten married to him. Fate intervened and protected her, but left her with a broken heart.

As I listened to my mom tell her story about her relationship with Ben, I can tell that there is still a question lurking in her mind: *Why did Ben just stop speaking to her for no reason?* Over sixty years later, she still has difficulty comprehending that it was mental illness that stole Ben from her, and it had *nothing to do with her*. I sense that my mom thinks there was something wrong with her that caused the breakup in some way - a pattern of thinking that has haunted her for her entire life.

As I learn more of my mom's history, I can see that she has had layers of feelings of abandonment and grief throughout her life. This layering began when she was sent away as a child to live with her grandmother, and then being sent away to boarding school. Being jilted by Ben and not understanding why it occurred was a painful loss for her because once again, she was feeling unwanted, unloved, and abandoned by those who were supposed to care for her and about her.

There was another large photograph of a handsome young man in mom's photo albums, and of course, curious me wanted to know who this guy was too. This picture was

"Jack," another suitor from my mom's younger days.

I learned more about Jack while spending time with my mom and her girlfriends when I would chauffeur them to Sunday mass after they were too old to drive themselves. We would have breakfast at Perkins after church, and it was during those times I would hear these women tell stories about Jack, when he was the main topic of conversation around the table.

I seriously doubt that Jack had any inkling that these women were still swooning over him sixty years later, but if I ever have the chance to meet him again, I will definitely let him know that he was the *"bee's knees"* to these women back in the day!

When Mom talks about Jack all of these

years later, I can still see the love in her eyes - the look of *first love*, which never really dies. When I did finally meet him briefly several years ago, I could see how she would have been smitten. He is a very handsome and friendly man with gentle manners and a kind smile.

Recently, I asked her to tell me more details regarding her relationship with Jack. She said that they had dated quite awhile and then he went into the military service. They would write letters back and forth when he was away, and to this day, she still has a ring that he gave her at that time.

She said he never mentioned marriage, so she did not think the ring signified any type of engagement. I can see where my shy, insecure mother, would never presume anything about the ring in case she might misread intentions that were not there.

It was during Jack's absence that she met Ben. Mom says that she was probably "carried away by the uniform" when she met Ben on that streetcar.

Her engagement to Ben required her to do the right thing and write to Jack, letting him know she had found someone new in her life and was engaged. It was a *Dear John* letter that I am sure my shy, innocent mother felt terrible writing.

Mom and Jack never spoke about their breakup and each went on to live their lives with new relationships and raising families. Jack married a wonderful woman who had been a housemate of my mom's when they both rented rooms at the same boarding house as single young women.

Today, my mom says she is so happy that he found a good woman and had a great life, but I also sense that there are some lingering feelings that reside inside my mom's heart for this man that she loved so long ago.

Knowing my mother, I believe that she still holds a bit of guilt for breaking off her relationship with Jack, and I imagine the awkward ending to her engagement to Ben left her with a heart that was fractured. Guilt and sorrow would be feelings my mother would carry throughout her life.

After two romantic heartbreaks, I am not sure my mom was really up for "falling in love" again, and in all honesty, I don't think she ever felt for my dad what she felt for those first two loves of her life.

My parents met after my dad arrived back in the States from Germany and France where he was stationed during World War II. Mom doesn't recall how they first met but believes it was during a time when groups of young women and men would go to dances at a local ballroom. I imagine my dad was quite hard to resist with his wide smile and sparkling, charismatic personality. Everyone loved being in the company of my dad, Harold.

My parents were poster children for the old adage *"opposites attract."* The outgoing, funny, *live-life-to-the-fullest* personality of my dad was definitely a direct opposite of my mother's shy, reserved ways.

I find it interesting that my mom has very

clear memories of dating Jack and can talk in great detail about how she met Ben, but she doesn't recall anything specific about how she ended up engaged to my Dad. I wonder if the years of pain and sadness that occurred prior to and during their marriage covered up her memories of those early courtship years. Or perhaps it was just a non-descript relationship, a relationship where mom just went with the flow, doing what she thought was expected of her, which was getting married and raising a family.

As that young child up in the attic, I loved looking at my parent's wedding album; the beautiful petite bride and the handsome, grinning groom. I would look at those pictures and want to know everything about that young couple, the young couple that would later become my parents.

However, one must be careful when searching for answers to relationships and lives of long ago, because the answers may not be what one hopes for.

For example, I always found it interesting that my mom has shared with me - more than a few times - that her father looked at her and said, "You don't have to do this if you do not want to," as they were standing in the back of church waiting to walk down the aisle on her wedding day.

I think Grandpa Schmitt's intuition was probably spot on. He knew that the marriage was not one of true passion and deep love. I think my mom probably knew it, too, but was too afraid to call it off at that late hour.

Our early interactions with those we loved, can shape who we become... we need to take care and interact with love and affection in all of our relationships... to allow everyone's light to shine brightly from within.

★ ★ ★

Chapter 6

The Book of Harold

My dad was born into a family that had a pretty big secret, a secret that was never revealed until he was an adult.

On his birth certificate, it says that he was *the first child of the mother,* but he had an older sister named Eleanor. Eleanor always lived with my Dad's maternal grandmother, Great Grandma McCaffery. Eleanor had the Huss family last name, and apparently my dad and his siblings never thought it odd that she did not live with them and their parents.

My grandmother waited until her children were adults before she told them that Eleanor was not my grandfather's biological child. She was born when my grandmother was 17 and briefly married to another man. Grandma apparently shared the details with her adult children, and after that time, it was never spoken about again. The story was buried, along with my grandmother and her children many years ago.

The only stories and information I gathered about my Dad's younger years were from sitting with him and his best friend, Dick Mertz, when they shared stories over coffee and donuts at the local bakery, a regular morning ritual when they got older. The stories were filled with laughter as they talked about the crazy antics of being young boys in a small town.

They were both fun-loving young men, and their friendship spanned many decades before my dad died. After both were married, their young families even shared a duplex, living next door to each other, and the men continued some of their crazy antics as next-door neighbors!

There was one particular story that Dick loved to tell with great glee. Apparently there was a connecting door between the interior of the duplexes from the basement. Dick had a great sense of humor so he decided to hang a calendar with a picture of a pin-up girl in my parent's home in a pretty prominent position.

When my parents arrived home, they just so happened to have the local priest in tow with them! Dick said he had to run like crazy, get over to my parent's side of the house and take down the calendar before the priest got in the house! I can only imagine the hysterical laughter he and my dad had when Dick first told him what happened! I am pretty sure they are laughing in Heaven about it right now as I type this!

Dick had married a super smart young woman named Pat, who also lived in that same boarding house my mom lived in. As you will see later in this book, it is interesting how the relationships of these people weaved in and out of each other's lives over the years.

Dad was an active youth, playing football in high school and was also a member of the town's local baseball team when he was a young man for before he got married. He was a confident and handsome guy who bore an Army uniform proudly as a Captain in the United States *Army Corp of Engineers*. He served in World War II, landing in Europe a few days after D-Day and the invasion of Normandy.

When my dad returned home from the war, he went to college for about a year and a half and then quit for some reason. I think it was costly and he was a social guy, probably not disciplined in getting the most out of college.

He and my mom eventually married, and he worked in his father's foundry for a time until he became a small business owner and purchased a *Mobil* gas station in his hometown.

I don't know much about his life during high school, or whether he had any girlfriends. He didn't talk much about that part of his life with me. I wish I had been more curious about Dad and his early years, but I never felt the need to get to know him better.

My dad and I had a connection that was deeper than words. I knew him. I knew what made him tick. I knew him at a deeper soul level. I knew him so much better than I knew my mom. I am not sure why there was such a difference in my relationships and connections with my parents, but it was just that way.

Dad was well known for his generosity to those in need and also as the guy who was always the *"life of the party"* with his humor and *joie de vivre.* He was so well liked in his community that he served one term as Mayor, and my parents became Shakopee's *First Family,* an all American middle class couple with two small children and another one on the way. Or at least that is how it appeared.

I recall a photo of my parents and older brothers from a newspaper article about the Mayor and Shakopee's *First Family* celebrating Easter. I never knew until interviewing my mother for this book that she was pregnant in that photo. She was carrying my brother Mike at the time, three years after my parents lost their baby boy, Greg. The picture shows my mom as a proper young wife, standing beside her husband, not smiling, just poised for the camera.

As I think about my family at that time, I imagine any holiday was painful after my brother Greg had died, and photographing the family for that Easter "Mayoral" photo was probably not one of joy but one of duty for my mom.

Our relationships with our parents can vary... we may feel more in tune with one parent versus the other. This doesn't make either relationship any better or any worse and it doesn't mean that there is less love for one than the other. It just means the connection is different.

Chapter 7

The Book of Gregory

It was during one of those times up in the attic as a little girl that I came across a five by seven inch manila envelope. I remember carefully opening the metal clasp and pulling out two black and white photos. The photos were of a baby in two different poses, and the baby just didn't look right; it was something in his face.

My curiosity was piqued. *Who was this baby?* He didn't look like any of my brothers' baby

93

pictures. *Why would my mother have two pictures of some baby that wasn't one of her kids?*

I don't remember if my mom came upstairs to see what I was up to, or if I took that manila envelope and pictures to her, but I do recall that I asked her, "*Who is this sick looking baby?*" She told me that the pictures were of my brother Gregory, who died when he was a baby.

That was the day that I met my brother.

I was so amazed that I had another brother. It was surreal for me to learn that there was another person in our family. I think it must be similar to the feelings of someone who has been adopted upon finding out that they have another set of parents and other siblings somewhere out in the world.

94

What was Greg like? What would he have been like if he would have lived? Would he and I have been close? Would he have Mom's reserved and quiet personality, or Dad's outgoing, exuberant persona? Would he have looked like my brothers, Steve and Mike (who always look so much alike as young children), or would he have looked more like my brother Dave, with the "olive colored" skin tone?

I knew I didn't look like Greg because I was the blond-haired, blue-eyed child who never felt like she really *belonged* in this dark-haired family of boys.

From that day when I first saw his pictures, Greg became a major part of my life. I learned that he was born on June 21, 1952 and died in October of that same year, from what my parents were told at the time was "pneumonia," but my mom believes it was a reaction to some injections he had received earlier on the day of his death.

My mom told me that those two pictures were the only pictures she had of Greg because he was so little when he died. She said someone took the pictures *post-mortem* at the mortuary so that my parents could have some pictures of him before he was buried. Pictures that also ended up buried away in the attic, in a little manila envelope.

Mom and I did not talk much more about Greg at the time I found his pictures, and his name was never spoken in our home. No one talked about Greg; not my mom, not my dad, none of my grandparents, aunts, uncles or any of my brothers. It was like he had never existed.

But Greg did exist...

I felt so close to him and I never understood or could explain why I was so connected to a brother that I had never seen except in those two photographs - until that *epiphany* happened to me on the plane three years ago.

As a young child, my curiosity of where I came from, and my brother, Greg, would draw me to the cemetery, where I could spend time being in his "presence." As a little girl in grade school, I would ride my bike to the cemetery and "hang out." I would peer down at Greg's grave marker and read his name.

Gregory John Huss
June 21 – 1952   October 12

Seeing Greg's birthday engraved on that stone was extremely important to me, because I was born on the following day six years later.

I knew deep in my soul that there was something important about our birthdays being a day apart, but I really did not understand anything more than the fact that Greg and I were deeply connected somehow; differently than how I was connected with my other siblings.

I am fortunate to have a mother who has lived into her nineties. My mother is a woman who has endured unimaginable heartbreak but who soldiered on day after day, year after year. She is a woman who is now willing to talk at length about the child who was lost to her so long ago.

In 2012, Greg would have turned 60 years old. It was during this time that I was able to gather more information about this baby who was a critical member of our family. Mom needed to talk about Greg. She needed to remember this baby who was lost to her so long ago.

She took the little manila envelope out of the metal box that held her important papers. It was the first time since I was a child that I saw those pictures. As I looked at them, memories of my childhood and spending time in that attic came back full force, like they had just happened yesterday.

My mom has a hard time remembering specifics about Greg, and that saddens her because, as she tells me, she "*never got to know him because he was just a little baby*" when he died. I will share my thoughts on why I believe my mom does not have a strong recall of her baby boy later in my story.

Mom describes Greg as a fairly quiet baby, and her memories are of carrying him around as she went about her tasks of taking care of her three little boys.

Greg was the third live birth in our family. My mom had a miscarriage with her first pregnancy and then she went on to give birth to my oldest brother Stephen on her twenty-fifth birthday (July 5, 1949). On April 15th, 1951, she gave birth to David, and while he was still a baby in diapers, Gregory John Huss entered this world on June 21, 1952.

As I now look at the two pictures of Greg at his death, I see a baby with a head full of long, silky dark hair combed back. His forehead and eyebrows remind me of my brothers, Steve and Mike.

I see my brother Dave, and my dad, mirrored

in his closed eyes and nose. I find it interesting to see the physical similarities between Greg and all of my brothers, but I do not see any resemblance to me. Yet I am the one he chose to send his spirit into as part of his re-birth.

Per my mother, the name Gregory was given to him by my dad, after some Archbishop in the Catholic Church at the time. My dad always had a strong connection to the Catholic Church during his life. I cannot say that he was the epitome of what a "good" Catholic would act like, but his faith was deeply important to him. It makes sense to me that Dad named his child after a leader in the Catholic Church.

As I look upon the pictures of Greg, I notice the chills flowing through my body - the now familiar sign that I know his spirit is here with me as I write our story, the story of our family, and the story of who I came to this earth to be. It all begins on the night Greg died.

Yes, it is a story that begins with Greg's death; yet it is a story with no ending. As I began to write our story, other stories came to me through other families who also suffered through the loss of a child. This book truly began to be a book of healing before words were even put down on paper.

Chapter 8

Another Child Tucked Safely Away

I went to my first women's *retreat* in March of 2015. Again, this was way out of the norm for me, but it seemed so natural for me to sign up and drive two hours away from home to hang out with a group of women, most of them I had never met before. I cannot imagine what was going through my husband's mind when I told him I was going away for the weekend with people I did not know.

This was a retreat where twenty women came together and bonded as *Soul Sisters*, a group of women who came to learn and share our spiritual experiences. It was a time for all of us to share our stories if we were so inclined. It was when I first told the story of my brother, Greg, and my *epiphanies* that led to such a dramatic change in my beliefs and in my spirituality. A change that occurred that moment on the plane, when I knew Greg had been a part of me since the day I was born.

The first night of the retreat, I talked about finding the manila envelope with Greg's pictures when I was a kid - the unmarked plain manila envelope.

I also shared the actual photos, which was something I would have never done previously but I felt a safety and a love within these women. It just felt like the right time to share the pictures of the little baby who had died so long ago. I gained affirmation from these women that I was not crazy after several of them just looked at me and told me that they believed Greg reincarnated back to our family - through me.

I had never thought of the term *reincarnation* prior to that time. I was not well versed in the metaphysical and New Age beliefs so this was all new to me. All I knew was that Greg was "*reborn through me.*" Those were the words that came to me that day on the plane. When these women talked about reincarnation, I did not feel anything unusual because I knew all along that what they sensed was most likely true.

There was one woman at the retreat who I did not really spend much one on one time with, yet when I came home, I felt like I needed to reach out to her. She is a graphic designer, and I was looking for someone to develop a new logo for my coaching company. I wanted someone who could tap into my essence and my spirituality. Someone who could understand who I was and bring my vision to life in a logo. I felt this woman would be a good fit for this project because she is a sweet, kind, and beautiful soul. She has a soulful beauty that emanates from her inner core.

We met one afternoon to discuss my coaching business and ideas for my logo. This woman is not only a graphic designer but also a Reiki practitioner who is not only artistic but also highly intuitive - a perfect fit to create my desired logo that speaks of spirituality, transformation, and beauty - the logo of a butterfly - a symbol and vision that I have carried with me since I was a very young child.

During our initial conversation, this gal looked at me and said, "You are my inspiration." She took me by total surprise. *Me? I inspire this talented, beautiful soul? Why?*

She told me that she had a baby daughter who was one day old when she died many years ago. She said that after I told my story at the retreat about Greg and his pictures in the little manila envelope, she went home and took out a plain, unmarked envelope from her jewelry box, a plain envelope that held the pictures of her baby girl.

She said she began writing information on the envelope, because she realized that if she did not document this information and anything ever happened to her, no one would ever know about the child she bore so many years ago. She too had buried this child both literally and figuratively at the time of her death.

This act of unburying her child from the bottom of her jewelry box opened up a spiritual relationship between this momma and her baby girl. She now feels her daughter and connects with her in ways that are not of this dimension.

A few months after our first meeting, which was a couple weeks before Mother's Day, she shared that she was getting a message from her child. The message was to buy herself something "pretty" - an unusual message because this is not a woman who would randomly go buy herself something frivolous.

She said she received the message again, so she asked her little angel baby if she would help her find what to buy. She sensed her little girl's spirit saying, "*Yes, I will help.*"

My friend went on-line, and an image of a charm bracelet "for little girls" with a beautiful message popped up on the screen. She knew that was the gift she was to give herself, so she ordered it in time to receive this gift from her angel child for Mother's Day.

Just think, if my mom had kept Greg hidden in the envelope, his spirit buried forever, this woman may have never had the opportunity to open up her heart to the level needed to reconnect with her baby's precious soul.

I shared this story with my ninety-one year old mom and told her she is helping other mom's with her story. I acknowledged the great gift she and Greg are giving to others who may feel the need for permission to tell their stories.

It is never too late to reconnect with our loved ones who have passed. It merely takes the conscious decision to open our hearts and breathe in their spirit - to grant them permission to return to us through our thoughts, memories, and interactions with others.

Chapter 9

The Night that Greg Died

October 1952 was a turning point in my life. It was the night my brother, Greg, died. It was the time that changed the lives of every member of our family, including the two of us who were born after his death. As I have been asking questions of my mother about that time in her life, she can now talk about the day that Greg died with great detail; many facts finely etched into her memory, while others shaded and blurred as a result of trauma and grief.

113

The story begins when my mom took Greg to the family doctor so he could get his *"baby shots."* It wasn't until after she had gotten him home, when things started to go terribly wrong. She said the baby cried continuously, and there was nothing she could do to console him.

She described the horror stating, *"When his eyes rolled back in his head, I knew something was very wrong."* She called the family doctor, and he told her to bring Greg to the local hospital. The hospital was run by a local order of Catholic nuns, which is an important fact as you read further into my mother's story.

Mom said that Greg's doctor (a close family friend) told my parents that evening to go home and get some rest because it appeared that Greg's condition was stable. They did go home and it was in the middle of the night when the phone call came. Their baby had died. From that moment forward, the whole future of our family changed.

The events that occurred after my parents got the call that night were heart wrenching to hear as my mom shared her story. I only repeat it as a way to paint the picture of how this baby's death changed life dramatically for my mom, my dad, my siblings, and myself.

I do not think there is anyone to blame, but I do believe that there are things for all of us to learn - to learn how to "be" holding the light of compassion and love within our hearts for those who are facing the death of a loved one, especially the death of a child. The details are important because they are part of my mom's story, and her story deserves to be told.

This is a book of healing - not only for my mom, but also for the countless other parents who have had a child die. Every single parent has their story, and it is extremely important for them to be able to share their story so they can be heard, so they can give voice to the events that happened, and hopefully in some small way, to find healing.

This book's purpose is to help others find healing, by allowing the words to be spoken *out loud*, allowing the words to be heard, allowing those who speak to be understood.

Mom says that she and dad went to the hospital after they got the call in the middle of the night, and there he was, their tiny baby laying on a gurney in the hallway of the hospital - their tiny baby with no blanket covering his little body. The only word I can describe from my mom's description of walking into a hospital seeing her dead baby is *trauma*.

My mother started her journey into what we call **PTSD** (*Post Traumatic Stress Disorder*) that evening. My mom used the word "*heartless*" as she described that moment. She felt the nuns were heartless because of the way they left her baby out in the hallway and all alone.

I tend to think that the nuns had no clue of the pain they caused my parents that night. They probably had hardened their hearts as nurses, hardened their hearts to protect themselves emotionally from the heartache and pain that they most likely encountered on a daily basis at the hospital. Unfortunately, that single event compounded the trauma my parents endured from the news of the death of their child, and it made them feel like no one cared because of the scene they walked in on that night.

My mom's memories of that night are the remaining ashes from the long ago fire of anger - a fire that raged when the nuns did not honor her child by caring for his little earthly body. The hurt and anger still remain smoldering under those ashes to this day, sixty-three years after the fact.

The ashes of hurt stem from comments made by others, such as the comment someone said to her after Greg had died, stating he *"thought he (Greg) always looked sickly."* That comment still hurts her because my mother had never noticed anything wrong with her child prior to the day he died.

The flickering flames of anger continue to burn from the fact that the local priest told my mom that Greg did not need a funeral (because he was a baby), and so her child's body was taken directly to the cemetery from the mortuary, with no ceremony to grieve over his loss.

Any grieving parent can tell you that the lingering red-hot coals of pain and anger can remain deep under the soot and ashes long after the death of a child. Certain memories re-ignites that flame, flickering brightly for a minute or two, before quickly being buried under the charred remains of the fire.

One of my client's, Cindy, came to me for coaching because she was having difficulty moving through the grief after the death of her father. As we began to talk, she soon shared with me that her middle daughter, Angie, died at the age of seven after a crush injury when she was playing.

Angela (Angie) Clow

2ⁿᵈ Grade Class Picture

121

Her daughter died over thirty years ago and the pain, anger, and guilt were still lying just under the surface of her emotions. Her father's death and his funeral brought back all of the traumatic memories of the time her little girl was accidentally killed.

She describes the pain that she endured at the time of her child's death as a "crushing chest pain." A pain that was more of a physical pain versus an emotional one; a pain that felt like her heart had literally blown apart and fractured into a million pieces.

Chapter 10

The Funeral That Wasn't

My mom said she was going to have a mass said for Greg when he died. Her words to me were: *"I did not care if I was the only one who showed up, I was going to have a mass for my child!"*

My mom - the shy one, the quiet one - could be a very intimidating mother bear when it came to her cubs, and if she felt anything was a threat to her children, nothing would stop her from protecting them. Having the priest tell her that she did not need to have a mass for her baby was one of the most extreme threats she ever faced in her life. Greg mattered. His short life mattered, and she was damn well sure she was going to have a mass for him.

She says she set up the mass, and then my dad's sister called Mom and told her that she felt that the mass should not be said for Greg, but should be said instead for my dad's grandmother, who had recently passed. My aunt also said the same thing to my mom as the family priest did: Greg *"...didn't need a mass because he was just a baby."*

"Just a baby."

Not having a ceremony for Greg was unthinkable in my mom's mind, and I believe rightfully so. How can anyone leave their loved ones without some time to say a proper good-bye?

It seems incomprehensible that my mom was being pushed to not have a funeral mass for her child. *Why? Was it because it was felt all children go to Heaven? Was it because the thought of going to a funeral for a baby was too emotional, too much to bear? Were they trying to protect Mom? Where was dad during this time? Why didn't he speak up and defend his wife's position on having a mass?*

There are still many unanswered questions, but I choose to believe that everyone who said something at that time said it out of compassion for my mom. It just was not received that way.

I learned just how important ceremony is at the time someone dies when our nephew.

Coleman, from my husband's side of the family, died. My brother-in-law chose to have a traditional Native American ceremony as Coleman transitioned into his next life.

Coleman died when he was eighteen years old, three weeks shy of graduating from the high school on the reservation where they lived. He died unexpectedly after suffering hypothermia when he was out celebrating with his friends.

After his death, his body was dressed in his traditional dance costume and laid upon a structure made by my brother-in-law. The Chief of the tribe had his Tipi erected on my brother-in-law's property so that Coleman's body could lie within the Tipi for the days of mourning.

His body was never left alone. The community of people brought gifts for Coleman. The tables surrounding his body were filled with pictures of his life, food to sustain him on his journey and cigarettes (tobacco), as was the custom. All to honor his spirit's journey.

The drummers came in the evening to do their drumming. The sound of the drums created an eerie yet peaceful energy floating through the air. Drumming - the sounds so varying, soft as a resting heartbeat, thunderous as a raging storm - so symbolic of the emotions that move through our hearts as we grieve the death of someone we love.

On the fourth day, the *Wiping of the Tears* ceremony was held at the high school gymnasium of this small reservation in South Dakota. The community came out in full force to pay their respects to our family. It was amazing and humbling to be sitting among the tribe, fully supported by all. The energy surrounding us was palpable; the energy of hearts connecting in a circle of healing during this time of death.

As we sat in chairs in the middle of the gymnasium, each and every person in that building came forward to individually shake each of our hands as a gesture of respect and honor for the family of this child who died. No words were spoken. A mere handshake and a bowing of the head spoke more to our hearts than any words ever could have.

The *Wiping of the Tears* ceremony is held on the fourth day of the wake and is the time to allow the spirit of the deceased to move on, to not be tethered to this earth by the tears and intense sorrow of those that remain. We needed to wipe away those tears so we could allow Coleman's spirit to be released into the universe to continue on his soul's journey.

Ceremony surrounding death is very important in most cultures. Having some type of ritual for saying good-bye to our loved ones is important for the living to deal with their grief. The ceremony also allows the grieving loved ones to be surrounded by the compassionate and loving energy of family and friends who want to support them.

Part II

Life After Death

Chapter 11

Grieving Greg

My mom still holds great guilt and heartache because she left Greg alone at the hospital. The questions she asked during our discussions were not directed to me but ones she asked herself: "*What kind of mother leaves her child at the hospital... what kind of mother was I that I would go home? what was I thinking? I should have been there and held him.*" It was then that the heart of the questions came out in this simple statement:

"I never got to hold him."

She never got to hold Greg after he died, not when she and Dad went back to the hospital, and not at the funeral home. I can see in her eyes that her arms still ache over sixty years later because she never got to hold her baby again.

I think we take for granted how much loving human touch really impacts us. I recently read somewhere that hugging someone for thirty seconds increases those "feel good" hormones in our bodies. Hugging calms us. It fills our hearts with love for both the giver and the receiver. Being unable to hug our loved one after their death robs the grieving from being able to physically release the overflowing love from their hearts into the soul of that person they love so dearly.

My mom talks of Greg's little arms being frozen in position and she questions how long he had been dead before the hospital personnel called my parents. She sees his little arms as reaching out, as a baby wanting to be held. My mom's guilt once again rears its ugly head for not being with her child when he died.

I have the sense that Greg was reaching out to the Light - you know, the beautiful white light that those with Near Death Experiences see - the light of **Heaven,** the Light of **God.** I know in my heart that Greg did not transition alone. I know he had loved ones waiting for him.

I know my mom's grandmother was there, the grandmother who had nurtured my mom and her sister during their younger years. I know she was there to take my mom's child into her arms.

My Great-Grandmother McCaffery was also waiting on the other side, along with my Dad's sister Eleanor, and our cousin Bobby. All those who had transitioned in the weeks before Greg's death were waiting with open arms for this beautiful child to arrive as his spirit left his tiny earthly body.

I also know in my heart that loved ones not only from our earthly family but also in our spiritual family greeted Greg. I am certain that he was taken into the arms of the one who is the epitome of motherly love, *Mother Mary*. I also believe that Jesus was standing right beside her, as Greg's spirit moved beyond the veil into the arms of Jesus. I mean, who else would be right there waiting for him

but the one who it is written and described as
"He who so loved the children?"

Mom doesn't recall much more surrounding Greg's death. She does not remember anyone coming to her home to console her, not her parents, not her sister, and not her friends. She mentioned once that her sister and friends didn't come because they were *"probably busy with their own families."*

However, Mom really wonders if it was because she was *"odd"* and that was why no one came to support her during this time of great loss. I find it interesting that my mom uses that term a lot. *"Maybe she was odd."*

I think she probably knows that she lost contact with her reality during that time, not unusual for most grieving parents. It is so difficult to grasp the realization that a child has died and I know from talking with many parents, they feel that a part of them also *dies* at the time of their child's death.

My friend Cindy, told me that she wanted to die right along with her child but told me, "*If I died, I chose to love her more (than her two living children),*" so she soldiered on.

Was Cindy "clinically" suicidal or was she just so deep into the initial grips of grief that her only thought was to be with her child? I imagine most parents who have experienced child loss have thought the same thing at least for a fleeting moment or two.

During that initial time of shock after the reality of death sinks in, a tidal wave of depression hits without warning and thoughts of living in a world without their beloved child is truly unbearable.

I am sure that my mom was immediately thrown into that shock and deep depression when her tiny child died so unexpectedly, so deeply in shock that she may not remember who came or did not come to console her. She recalls that people came to the mortuary, but when I asked if anyone came to visit with her at home after he was buried, she said no one came.

She does not remember anyone around to comfort her, no family or friends reaching out to give her a hug, or to sit quietly beside her. When I mention this to other people, they usually say something like, *"That is just the way things were handled sixty years ago."*

My brother Greg was laid to rest both literally and figuratively when he died.

As I mentioned earlier, no one ever spoke of

Greg after he died. My mom says that she and my dad never discussed Greg's death or their feelings; two parents in the tight grip of grief with no one
to talk to.

Recently I was talking to an old childhood friend whose son was accidentally killed over thirty years ago at the age of two. She said she remembers one of her children bringing up her son's name at the dinner table, and her husband immediately got up and left the room.

They were never able to speak of that tiny child who was an integral part of their family. The hole within the family fabric could not be mended by the colorful stories created with the threads of laughter or tears. The torn and ragged edges of that hole were never sewn together and thirty years later, the thinning and frayed threads disintegrated the fabric of the family.

Some marriages and families become stronger after the death of a child but there are many where the relationships within the family begins a slow painful death of their own, culminating in a myriad of dysfunctional behaviors including physical abuse, self-medication, divorce, or suicide.

Cindy speaks of how her husband self-medicated after Angie died, and the marriage became a toxic environment for them all. She finally left her husband, but not without creating a major tear in the fabric of their family.

In my family's case, my parent's marriage did not grow stronger...

Can you imagine being a grieving parent and no one reaches out to comfort you? Unfortunately, that scenario happens more frequently than we would like to admit. I call it the *Plague of Grief*. Many people are very uncomfortable discussing death, especially the death of a child.

In April of 2015, I was volunteering at the family grief camp and I talked to a dad whose son was killed in an accident. He told me that people treated him like he had some horrible, communicable disease. He said he *gets it* because people do not know what to say, but I could tell how alone he felt: He was an outsider, he was different, and he was from a minority group.

The minority group of **Grieving Parents**.

I also spent time talking with this man's wife and she said that she felt like she had a large *scarlet letter* on her chest and back, a sign advising people to stay away from her.

How sad is it that those in mourning sometimes feel abandoned by friends and family?

People retreat because of fear. Those who have not experienced the death of a loved one are afraid... afraid of saying the wrong thing, afraid to say something that might upset the person who is grieving.

In my mom's case, she was left feeling *"maybe I was strange and that is why no one talked to me."* It added another layer on top of the layers of sadness, anger, and guilt that she had already been experiencing.

Grief can leave us feeling like we are on an island by ourselves, trying to deal with the emotional angst that creates a deep physical pain in our hearts. An island built out of fear. I mean, *how can you say something that will provide comfort when dealing with the death of a child?*

I believe it is perfectly appropriate to not offerplatitudes to a grieving parent, spouse, or sibling who are reeling from the death of a loved one. We mean well when we say things like *"at least they didn't suffer," "they are in a much better place,"* or *"God needed them."*

I have heard from many grieving family members that the platitudes anger them at times. For them, it is not okay that the person died and nothing can make it feel right at that time in their initial grief.

146

However, it is okay to tell them that they have a right to their feelings of anger. It is okay to tell them that the rivers of tears flowing frequently down their face is normal. It is okay to speak of the loved one and actually use the name of the person who died. Grieving families want to talk about their loved ones to keep the memories alive and to honor their spirit.

Recently I gave a grieving grandma a *thinking of you and your family* gift bag of various items, angel figurines to represent the twin baby girls, the one who died and the one who survived. I included a photo of a butterfly as a way to symbolize her granddaughter whenever a butterfly flits by, and I gave her a journal to give Mommy and Daddy to write their personal thoughts in, if and when the time is right for them to do so.

The final gift was a heart shaped candle that I had burned at the *Hearts of Hope* camp that we had shortly after this child's death. A candle lit in honor of the beautiful baby girl who died so unexpectedly, a candle that her family can light when they want to reflect and remember their baby girl.

Did I upset this grandma by giving her this care package when she was in the initial throes of grief and disbelief?

No, I didn't. What I saw was gratitude in her eyes when I listened and she talked, when we spoke of her granddaughter by name. Gratitude that I was willing to share her memories and share in her pain, willing to hold her in love and comfort during this horrible time in her life.

I didn't think twice to create this "grief" bag. I just followed my instincts, knowing that if I were in her shoes, I would want someone to do the same for me.

I encourage you to think about how you would want you, your family or friends to be treated if tragedy struck within your own circle, then go out and "be" what you would like others to "be. I guarantee that your instincts will guide you to the right words and the right gestures.

Silence can be a powerful support, as long as you sit or stand in silence with the grieving person. Hold their hands, give them a hug, and put your arm around their shoulders.

Chapter 12

Compounded Grief

My family suffered great tragedy in the weeks leading up to the time of Greg's death.

First, my cousin Bobby died unexpectedly from a ruptured appendix on a Saturday. He was twelve years old. A few weeks later, Bobby's mother, (my Dad's half-sister, Eleanor), died unexpectedly from an aneurysm, leaving a husband, two very young twin boys, and her grandmother to grieve her death. She also died ***on a Saturday***.

Shortly after Eleanor's passing, my dad's grandmother died. Great Grandma McCaffery, who had been living with my Aunt Eleanor and her family, was the third person in that home who died **on a Saturday**.

I wonder if Eleanor and my Great Grandmother died from broken hearts after Bobby's untimely death? Maybe the stress and sorrow from the death of this beloved twelve-year-old child caused those two to follow shortly after.

It was after these three deaths, when my brother Greg died unexpectedly after getting his baby shots. Unbelievably, he also died **on a Saturday**. My mom says, *"I didn't want to answer the phone on a Saturday because I was so afraid someone else had died."*

I often wondered why no one came to my

mom and dad to give them the love and support grieving parents need, and it dawned on me recently that my dad's mother, Grandma Huss, lost two grandchildren, her daughter and her mother all within a matter of weeks. Grandma Huss was so deep in her own grief, I am sure that there was no capacity within her to console her son and his wife after their baby died.

So many people, so many broken hearts; profound grief engulfed my family.

My journey these past few years has brought me to meet other families with compounded grief. Stories of experiencing sibling death as a child, to only finding themselves having the same experience their parents did, the death of a child.

In Cindy's case, she was a young child, just

three years old, when her brother Murray (age eighteen months old), accidentally drank *Oil of Wintergreen* and died. For years, she held guilt because she had been playing in that room and around the drawer where the oil was kept. She has wondered for over sixty years, if she may have unintentionally left the bottle open or out for her brother to find.

Sixty years of guilt for an imagined act that killed her brother, imagined because it wasn't true, yet our minds' eyes can see things in very different ways, and in her little three-year-old mind, she did something that caused her baby brother to die.

Then the horror of all horrors occurs in her life when her daughter, Angela, dies as a seven-year-old child due to an accident; the grief and guilt was layered on top of the grief and guilt from Murray's death.

As the young child of a sibling death, Cindy knew the pain her own mother suffered with the loss of her child and now had to watch as her mother re-experienced that grief by having her grandchild die, her mother knowing that she could not take away the pain in her child who was now immersed in the horrendous grief of child loss.

My friend Jill Stephenson lost her child, Cpl. Benjamin Kopp, an Army Ranger when he died from wounds suffered in Afghanistan in 2009 at the tender age of 21.

Jill was also a sibling of a child who died. Her brother was killed in an accident when they were kids. She knew the toll grief took on her parents and her family only too well, and then she experiences that grief more intimately as this single mom learned that her only child was declared brain dead after he underwent surgery for his wounds.

Jill talks about sitting next to her mother at Walter Reed hospital, when the doctors gave them the news that Ben was only being kept alive by machines and his brain was not functioning. She said she got angry for only a few minutes and asked God, *"How could this happen to two mothers in the same family?"*

She said she then looked over at her mother and realized that Ben's death was not just about her, but also about her mother. It was then she made the choice to not carry anger with her over the death of her child, but to make certain that his life mattered, going forward by making a difference in the lives of others.

Compounded guilt, compounded anger, compounded grief - it happens far more frequently than most of us can imagine.

Jill Stephenson and Cpl. Benjamin Kopp

Chapter 13

A Mother's Guilt

I have talked to many parents who have suffered the death of a child and a common theme is that they feel guilt for what they "should" or "should not" have done. My mother's guilt has been imbedded in her for over sixty years.

My mother shared with me that she felt guilty when Greg became sick that day because he cried uncontrollably and she tried desperately to calm him down, but his crying would not subside. As she recounted that day, she looked up at me with eyes that still carry great pain. She told me that she had this little baby in her arms, held tightly against her chest as she was pacing back and forth, when she shook him slightly, desperately asking him, *"Why won't you stop crying?"*

She did not shake him hard, she did not shake him out of anger and she certainly did not shake him to cause him harm in any way. She was a young, twenty-eight year old mother; panic-stricken because she could not console the child she loved. She was worried sick that day and reacted like any frightened young mother would, given the same set of circumstances.

Unfortunately, holding that little baby tightly and shaking him in her arms, as he was inconsolable, is a lasting memory imprinted in her mind.

My friend who's two year old was accidentally killed, shared with me how she had her child in her arms after the accident and then she "threw" him into her husband's arms and ran away. Her husband did not understand how she could run away, and to this day, I can tell that she also questions why she did what she did.

As a grieving parent, immediate reactions are not carefully thought out, but are born out of the instincts of fear - fight or flight. My mom was trying to fight to calm down her baby. My friend needed to flee because it was too much to see her tiny child broken.

The second piece of Mom's memory, pushing her into a sixty-year guilt trip, was leaving Greg at the hospital that night and not being there when he died.

Greg's doctor, who was a close family friend, told my mom and dad to go home and get some rest, so they did. Back in the 1950's, physicians were held in highest regard and total trust. It is understandable why mom and dad went home that night, because someone they trusted told them they should.

Years later, that same physician told my mom, *"Ruth, if I had any idea at all that he (Greg) was going to die, I would **never** have told you to go home that night."* I cannot imagine the horrible guilt our doctor had after that night. He encouraged my parents to leave with the best of intention, and the end result was the worst possible scenario.

Knowing that Greg was having seizures at home before being hospitalized, there was a distinct possibility that Greg may have had further seizures that night, or he may have struggled with his breathing, possibly gasping for breath at the time of his death.

I am not sure what would have been harder on my mom, watching her baby struggle and take his last breath, or not be there at the time of his death. I imagine that if she had been at the hospital at the time of his death, she would have had guilt for not being able to save him.

I believe my parents were not meant to be at the hospital the night Greg died. I believe that circumstances occurred the way they were supposed to be played out. They were not at the hospital because God wanted to protect them from the trauma of watching their child die.

Guilt is a natural human emotion as part of the grieving process. However holding the guilt in without sharing it with someone safe to confide in will not allow the emotional healing process to occur. Speaking our guilt out loud allows the guilt to move from within us out into the universe so that we can let it dissipate into the air.

Chapter 14

A Father's Unspoken Grief

My dad was a wonderful man. His charismatic personality and joy of life drew people in. He was funny, with a smile on his face and a twinkle in his eye. He was the consummate politician who everyone liked. He was kindhearted and generous.

He also was an alcoholic.

Dad spent much of his time away from the house when I was growing up. When I was

171

very young, he ran a local gas station and is well remembered for his kindness and always wanting to help people out. He successfully ran for his first stint as a County Commissioner when I was in grade school, but when he ran a second time and lost, it seems as if his life started to plummet out of control.

He worked in sales and as a real estate agent, perfect career choices for this outgoing guy. He was really smart, but always seemed to struggle to make money to support his family.

His drinking became more problematic when I was middle school age, and by the time my brother Mike, three years older than me, graduated from high school, my mom had decided to relocate with her employer because she needed to make sure she had a home and money to raise me through high school. I will go into more detail about that period of my life later on this book.

I don't recall spending much time with my dad while I was in high school: a few visits here and there but nothing of substance that I can remember. I was too busy being a wild teenager in my new surroundings, and Dad was unable to focus on me because he was dealing with his own issues of self-medication for whatever was causing him to not be healthy or happy.

I believe that Dad's journey into alcoholism was exacerbated by the death of his child.

As I was writing this chapter of the book, I told my Dad that I needed to "channel" him, because he has been dead for twenty-five years and I really felt the need to hear his story. Now, I am new to this entire *channeling spirit* thing, but I knew I had to open my mind and my heart and listen carefully to whatever came to me from my dad.

The following is part of a silent conversation I had with him one evening. It was a stream of questions and thoughts flowing through my brain and onto the paper. I really had no conscious thoughts of what I was writing at the time, which leads me to believe that Dad was sharing his thoughts with me that night. The questions written down were really his way of guiding the conversation so that I could understand how he felt during his life.

I have highlighted the areas that I feel were his answers to me through my writing:

Q: *"Dad, how did you feel?"*

This tiny baby lifeless, my flesh and blood, another little Huss boy with tiny fingers and hands... he has my eyes. I named him Gregory John after an Archbishop...

It hurt too much to talk about Greg. My nephew, my sister, my grandmother, and then my baby boy... all gone within a matter of weeks.

I cannot console my own mother. I cannot console my wife.

Q. Were you angry? Did you blame your friend, Doc Ponterio? Did you blame Mom?

I blamed myself for not being a "hands on" dad... I blamed myself for not supporting your mother... I don't blame your mother and I do not blame Jim (Dr. Ponterio).

I feel so bad for Mike because it seems like he was the lost one. Mom coddled him out of fear. Mike was the adventuresome one and so much like me in so many ways, but I did not spend as much 1:1 time together that I wish I would have. We would have had a lot of fun together if I hadn't been so wrapped up in my own stuff.

Q. Did you know that Greg's spirit was born again through me? I have the sense that you were that intuitive...

I knew the day that you were born there was something special about you... it was more than being our little girl. I felt complete when you were born in a way that I had not felt since Greg died... You came along and were Daddy's little girl... someone I could shower my love on... someone who could help me feel joyful again... for at least a little while...

After awhile, I filled my life with activity away from home; I spent time with friends and comrades. It was too difficult to be home. To nothave the family I dreamed of because a hole was left in the middle of our family. I never really talked with my friends about Greg. There were a few of us men who probably should have shared about the deaths of our children but it was just easier to not talk about it... to not think about it.

You never spoke of Greg and the only time I saw you acknowledge his being was when we went to the cemetery and I showed you how his stone was sinking into the earth. You immediately set forth to find someone to raise it up with cement.

I never visited his grave. It was just too hard and a painful reminder...

I remember having to cut away the earth to uncover his stone when I went to visit him after many years
away. It was so important to me that Greg's marker be visible... to be honored.

It was hearing from you that Greg's marker was buried under the earth for me to finally go visit my son's resting place and it was not long after that when I was put to rest right beside him...

Dad, I am so sad... sad for you and Mom and the horrible grief you both encountered when your child died so unexpectedly.

I am sad that joy was gone from our lives. I am sad that our family died to some extent when Greg died. Life on earth at the time seemed as if it would never be without grief again...

I tried to keep things going by getting involved in my business and the community but I slowly lost my hold on my health and my love of life slowly deteriorated... Steve left, Dave left, Mike graduated, and then Mom and you left...

I did not make the greatest of choices while I was on earth and for that I am sorry... I am sorry because I did love all of you so much... your mom, Steve, Dave, Mike and you... but I was deep into my own self-destruction and I was stubborn... too proud to admit it.

The path you walked on this earth was not easy yet you remained a faith-filled man until the end.

St. Mary's church was my sanctuary and it was that Faith that allowed me to move from my earthly existence with the confidence that my next journey would be a good one. I wasn't afraid to die... in fact I welcomed it, and that is why I chose to not treat the cancer and just let my physical body go, so I could live in this beautiful after-life.

I had Faith that I would be welcomed into Heaven... I knew there was nothing that God would not forgive me for.

I had to learn a lot while I was in human form and it wasn't easy. The strokes, the inability to talk clearly, and losing my family, my friends and my home, were all very bad times for me. I know that I am the one who made bad choices but it honestly wasn't to hurt anyone... I was just too deep into my own alcoholism and pride.

The great thing about death is that it gives way to life... I was able to move into this beautiful existence free of physical, emotional and mental pain. I am whole again... I am happy... I can love freely...

I am also never far away from any of you. I want you, your brothers and your mother to know that I am always by their side even though they do not see or feel me. I am here for all of you unlike what I was like in my human form.

I also want all of you to know that all is forgiven when we die... we do not suffer in Heaven... God loves all of us and embraces all of us and never judges us harshly for what we did on Earth... He only wants us to understand unconditional and overwhelming Love and Peace. Trust me and know that death is new life... not an ending but just a beginning.

I know your mom is having difficulty understanding and believing right now... just keep loving her. She will soon find that all of her insecurities, guilt and sorrow will be forgotten once she leaves her earthly body. She will actually <u>BE</u> the joy that has eluded her for so many years during her earthly lifetime.

Go forward and tell our story, do not be stopped by fear of saying something you shouldn't. I want you to write it freely because this book will help others and that is what your role is now... to be the conduit by connecting others to the light of Faith, Comfort, Peace, and Love that resides within every soul.

Know that Greg and I fully support you. Know that all of us who love you are surrounding you with our love and our approval for what you are doing. Know that when you feel those familiar sensations and we come to your thoughts, we really are right there beside you...

Chapter 15

The Greatest Gift

I have never talked to my two oldest brothers about Greg, but Mom says that she has asked them and neither Steve nor Dave remember Greg or that period of time after his death. That makes sense due to the fact that Steve was just a young child of three years old, and Dave was only nineteen months old when Greg died.

My brothers may not remember their little brother or the changes in the energy of their home after his death, but I am certain that when Greg died, everything changed for them. Mom tells of becoming deeply depressed and feeling so very alone.

I can only imagine the change for these two small children... one day being a part of a typical suburban family, and the next day living in a home clouded in shadows and darkness. One day they have a baby living in their house and then all of a sudden that baby is gone.

I wonder who took care of them the days after Greg died?   Did Mom just go through the motions of cooking, feeding and bathing them or did someone come and make sure they were looked after?

As I said earlier, Mom does not recall anyone coming to help her, so did this mean that Steve had to learn at the age of three to take care of his little brother and himself?

Steve and Dave have always been close with one another. Their ages were fairly close at fifteen months apart, so they hung out with many of the same friends and had a relationship that Mike and I never had with them.

I think their relationship became more bonded when Greg died. They were two little boys who had a dramatic change in their home and they probably had to depend on each other for the emotional support and attention that both of them needed.

It was during this time, that my mother was granted a gift from a dear friend.

As I had mentioned earlier, my Dad's best

friend, Dick, married a gal who roomed with my mother when the two women were single. It was Dick's wife, Pat, who my mom credits being the person who broke her free from the tight grip of grief that had engulfed her after Greg's death.

Mom shared that she had lived in a fog after Greg died, and it wasn't until her friend Pat said to her, *"you need to snap out of this Ruth... you have two little boys who need you to take care of them,"* when the fog started to lift. That comment is what "woke" my mother up and got her to start living life again.

What a courageous and loving friend Pat was to speak the gift of *truth* to help my mother transition out of the darkness of depression and into the reality of living.

I found out recently from one of her children that Pat had a son who had died. Michael, her first-born child, was no more than six months old when he died. This would have occurred a few years before Greg was born.

I find it interesting that my mother doesn't remember Pat and Dick having a child named Michael, nor anything about them suffering through the death of their baby, yet it was Pat who was the only person who would have the courage and love for my family to speak up.

Pat had experienced what my mother was going through. She knew what it was like to grieve over the death of a child, and she also knew what it took to pull herself from the depths of sorrow and be *present* to give birth to, and raise, future children. Pat was clear that her children born after Michael, deserved love and attention from their parents regardless of the heartache from Michael's death.

I find it somewhat amazing that Pat was in my mom's life prior to either of them having children and that Pat suffered the loss of a child prior to my mom losing Greg. Was it just coincidence or was something greater at play?

I personally believe that Pat and my mom had a *Soul Contract* (which I will go into more depth later in this book). I believe they were destined to experience the death of a child in the pattern that it happened. Pat would experience the death of a child first so that she could be the one to bring my mom "mentally" back to life after she suffered the same type of loss.

Soul Contracts are those agreements we have made at the soul level to help each other experience life's lessons. To be courageous and speak the Truth honestly and gently from the heart is one of the greatest gifts we can give someone we love when they are in the grips of grief.

Our deceased loved ones never want us to fall into the grips of deep depression. They want us to find happiness in the beautiful memories and to live our lives with love and divine purpose.

After my mom's conversation with Pat, she buried her grief, much like they had buried Greg at the cemetery. She went back into her suburban housewife mode to raise her two young boys. Two young boys who most likely had no real clue what had happened, but who had to feel a deep change in the emotional atmosphere of their home.

I recently listened to a grieving mom question how she was supposed to handle Christmas after the unexpected death of her two year old. I asked my mom how she handled that first Christmas which occurred just two months after Greg's death.

She said that she felt it was important to give her children a Christmas that was memorable in a good way. She didn't think it was fair to not have Christmas for my brothers, because she felt Greg's death *"was not their burden to bear."* It is so very typical of my mother to carry the burden of grief all by herself.

It saddens me when I think of my family those months after Greg died. The sad mommy and daddy, and the two little boys who had no clue what happened. If only there had been some of the knowledge and resources like we have today to help children understand what happens when someone dies, and to help their parents in figuring out how to deal with their grief while still supporting their children.

The energy of a home changes dramatically when grief enters in. If someone you know is experiencing deep grief, take the time to bring the gift of light into their home. If they have young children, offer to take the kids for a few hours and allow the kids to have an outing filled with laughter and joy.

Chapter 16

Life After Sibling Loss

The memories I have of my two older brothers at home pretty much center around their picking on my brother Mike, born three years after Greg died. Some of the more memorable "fights" the boys had are ones that I question if my memories are totally accurate, but they were significant enough that they have stuck with me since I was a child.

Since Mike was four years younger than

Dave and six years younger than Steve, I think he was too young to hang out with them, and being the baby of the family for the three years before my birth, he was a prime target to be picked on by the older boys.

There was a period of time when I recall a hole being kicked into the basement hollow core door, an ear that needed to be stitched up after being hit against the kitchen counter, and a head dunking in the toilet when the two older ones ganged up on Mike.

I always thought that this was typical of the roughhousing that went on in a household of three rambunctious boys, but I wonder now, *"What would it have been like if Greg were alive? Would it have been more extreme fighting with four boys? Was the roughhousing in our home "normal" or was it tipping the edge of dysfunction?"*

As you have probably figured out, our parents were not home much during this time. My mom went back to work when I was five and had started kindergarten. This was a very different scenario than the way my older brothers were raised, when she didn't work outside of the home.

My memories of my oldest brothers from the time I was a young child are pretty limited. Steve is nine years older than me, so when he was in high school, I was just a little kid in early grade school. However, I do have a couple of specific memories of him taking care of me when I was a little girl.

I remember him having to clean me up (and the kitchen floor) when I was five or six years old and sick with the stomach flu. Here was this teenage boy, who calmly cleaned up the mess on the floor and then took me by the hand, guiding me back to my bedroom and getting me tucked into bed.

I also recall the time I froze my feet from ice-skating outdoors for hours and hours in the dead of winter, which in Minnesota means it was very cold! If you have ever frozen your feet, you know it hurts like heck when the sensations start returning and the nerves begin to have feeling again. The nerves feel like they are literally screaming and it is truly excruciatingly painful!

As I was screaming in pain, Steve came running into my room to see what was going on. I remember him kneeling on the floor as I sat on the edge of the bed, rubbing my feet to get the circulation moving. He seemed to have a natural instinct in knowing what to do to care for me.

Then there was the time that he literally saved my life. I was on the back steps sucking on a hard candy when it lodged into my throat. I ran panic-stricken into the house and Steve grabbed my little body, threw me on the kitchen table and pounded on my back until the candy flew out.

Being the eldest in our family, Steve assumed the role of caretaker. He was the responsible one with natural instincts, making sure I was always safe and taken care of while my parents were at work.

My brother, Dave, was the child who inherited my dad's personality and physical looks. Both my dad and Dave were endowed with charisma and a wonderful talent for story telling and humor. People have always been naturally attracted to their personality style.

They both could be the life of any party. Extroverts, like my dad and Dave, get their energy from being around other people. Dave is still very much that way to this day, and when he is around, there is never a lull in the conversation!

I am sure my mother would have preferred to stay home with us kids, but as I mentioned earlier, my dad had his struggles. He wasn't bringing home enough money to pay the bills, so a second income was needed to keep a roof over our heads, clothes on our backs, and shoes on our feet. Those responsibilities fell onto my mom's shoulders.

Caycie is a woman I know, who was not even two years old when her older sister accidentally died at the age of seven. She talked to me about how growing up in the midst of unresolved grief made her really angry. She was angry at her mom for being a "*basket case*" of depression, sadness, anger and guilt. She was angry that her dad turned to self-medication to deal with his emotions.

Caycie felt like she had to be the "adult" in the relationship with her mother when she was just a kid herself. She was angry that her parents' marriage failed after the death of her sister. She even told me that she would get angry with her dead sister. She was angry and blamed her sister for creating a life engulfed in parental despair.

Caycie said that having her own child helped her get over her anger with her mom. When Caycie's daughter was born, she finally understood. She understood what having a deep love for a child meant, and she understood her mom's tortured existence after the death of her child.

As I shared earlier, Cindy, Caycie's mother, had been a small child who took on the guilt of her brother's death for most of her life. Children who are around at the time of their sibling's accidental death can easily take on a cloak of guilt and responsibility for their brother or sister's death.

Another woman shared with me that she was a survivor from a car accident that killed her sister. She had carried "survivor's guilt" for years. This woman had not been responsible for the car accident and she was unable to save her sister's life, yet she carried the guilt for years until she found a therapist who had a spiritual side to her practice.

The therapist told her that she believed that when our souls depart our earthly bodies, it is because they have completed their journey in helping others experience what they needed to. The therapist told this woman that her sister gave her and her family "a gift" and "sacrificed" herself to help her family experience and learn from her death.

Their mother went forward to have more children because she felt a need and desire, knowing that she wasn't finished in her role as a mother. This person's birthplace among her siblings also changed with the death of her sister. She went from being the youngest in birth order, to being a middle child, and then ultimately being the oldest of the siblings.

I believe her life purpose was born from the tragedy of her sister's death, and now this woman is a nurturer of children and runs a daycare. She has become an extension of other family units while the parents are working. *I wonder if she would have created this life path had her sister not died when this woman was a young girl?*

Sometimes we will take on the responsibility for the death and allow guilt to surround us. Understanding that we are not responsible and that some divine purpose and learning does come out of death will help healing during grief.

Keith was a co-worker of mine who was willing to share his story for this book. In 1984, he was twenty-six years old when his younger sister, Kim, was severely injured in a car accident, leaving her in a coma before she died.

Keith recalls just being numb after Kim's death. As a young adult, he needed to step up and take responsibility for planning her funeral because his parents were simply not capable of doing so in their depths of grief. A total change occurred within the family dynamics.

He remembered that when the time came to make a decision on whether Kim's body should be used for organ donation, his mother was all by herself because his dad was out golfing, and she could not reach him to have a conversation on what decision they should make.

Keith stated that his parents wanted an open casket for family and friends to view Kim before the funeral. He talked about his "last image" of his sister stating that "she was unrecognizable" due to the injuries and trauma sustained from the accident. That image continues to haunt him to this day.

Keith tells of his mother experiencing great anger because she had taken his sister to a neurologist prior to the accident because she was having headaches. The neurologist basically told them that there was nothing wrong and then two weeks later, Kim suffered a brain aneurysm, which caused her to lose control of the car she was driving.

As the child who had to step in to be the

adult/parental figure overnight at that time, Keith never had time to grieve. It wasn't until seven years later when his paternal grandfather died that he could finally let go and grieve for his sister. He said he had a "relapse" and "relived" his sister's funeral all over again, only this time he really felt the pain and deep grief.

Keith's Dad, a retired military man, became withdrawn and had a difficult time talking about his daughter after she died, which I have found has been a fairly common thread of dealing with grief for men. Keith shared that his father still has never gone deep into his grief over the death of his young daughter.

Keith's mom became "anti-social" and for the first three years, she would not attend any family functions because the pain was too great for her. She also became "short and curt" in her verbal interactions with people. He described her personality as "anger oozing out of her body."

Thirty years later, Keith is still in the role as the head of the family. In one car accident, he went from being the oldest child to the only child. He handles the family affairs, including getting his parents acclimated to assisted living, selling their home, and watching his mother deteriorate with dementia.

As Keith can tell you, grief never goes fully away. He shared that his cousin's son died approximately ten years ago in a car accident. He says it once again brought back the painful memories of his sister's death.

As I have been writing this book, I have been honored to hear more stories from siblings and their experiences after the death of a sibling.

An old friend shared with me that when her sister was dying from leukemia when we were in grade school, she felt "invisible." She had two older brothers and a younger sister. As the middle child, she felt forgotten and left on the sidelines because her parents were naturally focused on her sister who was so ill. She said that she asked one of her brothers if he remembered her being around and he told her "no," he didn't recall anything about her at that time.

As a side note to the above story, I looked up from my desk in my home office while I was writing this page and there sitting on the shepherd's hook that holds some of our bird feeders, was a beautifully brilliant red Cardinal perched on top of the hook! This is the first Cardinal that I have seen by our feeders and I believe that my friend's sister is sending a message for me to let my childhood friend know that she has never been forgotten!

When parents are grieving, the remaining children can sometimes be inadvertently "forgotten" in the midst of the anxiety and grief or feel less important than the sibling who died. If you know anyone who is a sibling (regardless of whether they are younger or adults, take the time to specifically comfort them and let them know that they are seen and cared for.

Chapter 17

Born into Grief

Three years after Greg died, my parents brought another son into this world, my brother Mike. My mom says that she was extremely over-protective of him because losing Greg created a diligence within her to ensure Mike was safe and sound.

Poor Mom! Mike was the kid who was into everything, so her need to keep him safe was sorely put to the test at times! He was a risk-taker from a very young age, meaning, my mom had her work cut out for her to keep him out of danger!

Mike was the baby of the family for three years, totally coddled by an over-protective mother who still had grief in her heart that she had never able to talk through. It was not surprising then, when I came along three years after he was born, I unintentionally knocked him off of the pedestal as the *baby of the family.*

Being best of friends was not the way the family dynamics were going to play out between Mike and myself once I came into this world.

The memories I have of my childhood relationship with Mike pretty much center around us fighting. My smart-aleck mouth would say something that I knew would irritate him and off I'd run with him chasing after me. *Enemies* until something got broken, and then we would quickly become *partners in crime*, trying to fix whatever it was that we busted up during one of those infamous fights.

I think both of us were probably jealous of each other. Mike's jealousy stemmed from the fact that I came into the family and attention was take away from him, and my jealousy arose from being the baby in the family and wanting all of the attention of my parents and siblings focused on me.

Some of my childhood behavior towards Mike *haunts* me because I feel like I robbed my brother of my grandfather's loving energy. If we were out at my grandparent's farm and my Grandpa Schmitt was within earshot, I would scream out as if Mike was hurting me, when in fact he wasn't even sitting near me. My grandpa would then ask my mom from the other room, *"What is he doing to her?"* as I would sit smugly on the couch looking over at Mike like I had won the big war.

Poor Mike, picked on by his older brothers and then having this little *snot* of a sister who not only threw him under the bus whenever she could, but also made sure it drove solidly over him at times. No wonder he wanted to beat the crap out of me much of our childhood years!

I wonder what life with Mike would have been like if Greg had lived? I imagine our family dynamics would have been very different because Mike and I would have grown up in a home where our parents would not have been shrouded in shadows and grief.

Would we have been closer as the two younger siblings if Greg had not died? Would there have been more siblings in our family between Greg and Mike, or between Mike and I, versus the three-year spans that separated us?

I look back now and see that Mike and I lived a very different life than our older brothers. When Mike came into the family, I am sure my mother was a nervous wreck, with underlying fear and guilt from Greg's death, making her a totally different nurturer for Mike. Then I came along, and it rocked Mike's world, because mom had to devote time and attention to this new child brought into the family.

Interestingly enough, Mike and I have both had successful careers and even though we both lived a bit of the wild life back in the 1970's, neither one of us got stuck into unhealthy lifestyles that many of our friends fell victim to.

I think because of our birth positions in our family, and the fact that we were born into a grieving family, it gave us competitive spirits with each other because we were destined to be warriors, determined to fight our way into successfully taking hold of our place in our family and in this world as a whole.

Chapter 18

A Little Girl's Memories

I started writing this book in early 2015, and most of it came quite easily for the first several chapters, and then I lost the initiative and energy to continue writing.

The book was always in the back of my mind but it took me a few months of zero activity before I pulled it back up on my computer, and that is when I had the realization that I had to go deeper into my story, the story of how growing up in a home that had experienced the death of a child impacted me.

I knew that I had to reach into the core of my being to be able to share my story, including the feelings, the behaviors, and who I was as a child, teenager and young adult. I knew I needed to be honest in how I felt growing up in my home, but I was nervous to bring up my feelings; nervous because I was uncertain how my family might react to this book, to my story.

I know now that this is not just my mother's story, it isn't just Greg's story, and it isn't just my dad's story. This book encompasses all of our stories; the weaving together of everyone's story, creating the tapestry of our life. Each of our stories are beautiful strands creating colorful images against a backdrop of darkness, with the images taking shape in the fabric.

I found myself having to dig deep for understanding, to dig deep for forgiveness, to dig deep and be willing to be naked and exposed, with the hope my story will help others understand the impact unresolved grief can have on a family.

History is what helps tell our stories and I find it interesting that this is where I have been stuck. I don't have a lot of memories from my childhood, and I have always been the girl who likes to move forward and not live in the past.

In fact, I have been proud to be that person who doesn't constantly focus on the past, but I recently realized in an *AHA* moment, that history should not be shoved away on a shelf to sit forever unopened, layered with dust. History needs to be pulled out every so often, dusted off and re-opened to read words on those pages, to help us learn who we are and where we came from.

What I am learning as I have been peeling away the layers of myself for this book, is that there is a part of me that still needs to come to understand the impact the death of my brother has had on my life. There is some really awesome stuff that occurred in my life because of my experiences with death and grief, bringing me into my life purpose.

There are also areas of my life where I have to be honest, that it wasn't so awesome all of the time. I can use self-deprecating humor and act like it is not a big deal, but truth be told, there have been times in the writing of this book, where the tears fell as I rewound the tapes and hit "play", viewing those images of long ago.

The reality is, I grew up in a sad home. A home where there was flickering anger licking at the surface and a crumbling foundation that could not be seen with the naked eye.

I do have some vague memories of being a very young child. The first is one where I was a baby/young toddler. I remember standing up holding onto the crib rails, crying out loudly because I wanted someone to get me out of the crib.

Eventually my mother came into the room and picked me up, taking me out into the living room where there were a group of ladies sitting around. I remember some "*oohing and ahhing*" as the attention from the ladies focused on me, but what I remember the most is sitting on someone's lap, feeling ***happy and secure.***

As a person who really does not retain many memories of her past, it is interesting to me that I have this memory from such a young age and it is the only one of two memories where my mother came into my room to comfort me.

I don't remember being held or cuddled by my mother, but I am sure she did. I don't remember her tucking me into bed at night, but I am sure she did. I don't recall her giving me a kiss or a hug growing up, but I am sure she did.

I know my mom has loved me since the day I was born, but I think she put up an armored shield around her heart after Greg died as a way to protect her heart from ever being further shattered. I believe my mother could not fully expose her heart through cuddles and kisses after the loss of one of her babies. Her grief took away her ability to fully express herself in love.

I remember calling my mom when I was living and working in Colorado and had just finished going through *The Landmark Forum*, a program to help one move through barriers in their lives that stop them from leading fulfilling lives.

On this particular phone call, as we were saying good-bye and getting ready to hang up, I said, "*I love you Mom.*" It was the first time that I had said those words out loud to my Mom. It took me almost 40 years to make them real to her.

The silence on the other end of the line was

almost deafening. My poor mother did not know how to respond because being told that she was loved wasn't something she experienced as a child, so she was never taught to express her love this way as an adult.

I continued to tell my mom that I loved her after every conversation with her since that day in Colorado, and over time, she started telling me that she loved me back.

Years later, it is now a common sentiment that we express our love for each other in our family. My brothers and I freely say *I love you* to our mother and she does the same with us. Three little words that mean so much.

I LOVE YOU.
Keep these simple yet powerful words in your daily conversations with your family and friends. Speak them often to the Angels who surround you and help you as you walk life's journey. Speak them out loud, speak them with your eyes, and speak them with your smile...

When our older brothers were no longer living at home, Mike and I would fight like cats and dogs when we were alone in the house, but when my parents were home, our little family would live in the same house with no one really talking to each other. We read a lot, burying our heads in books, or Mike and I would go play quietly in our own separate worlds.

Mike loved working in a little room in the basement, concocting potions with his chemistry set and I would play quietly in my bedroom or be down in another area of the basement where we had a couple of antique school desks and a chalkboard. I would be the teacher with my dolls posing as my students, and I would teach them by writing on the old blackboard we had hanging on the wall.

I don't remember playing games as a family.

I remember Dad trying to bring us around the table to play some games or cards once in a great while, but our "family" time was pretty limited.

I had a dollhouse that was my favorite play item, probably because my grandfather made it for me. I would spend hours rearranging the miniature furniture and orchestrating how the family lived in that house. There was a baby who I could sit in the high chair and I remember taking great pains in feeding that little baby, nurturing that little play figurine, pretending to be its mommy.

I liked having the whole family in this miniature home together where I would have conversations in my head creating what they all would be saying to each other. Clearly, my play was an attempt to create a close knit family; something very important to me because even at a young age, I sensed my real family was not a super happy family. We were a family that resided in the stillness of life that was not really being lived.

I would also play with the box-elder bugs that crawled the stucco siding of our house by naming them and pretending that they were a family bustling about their lives as they scurried up and down the side of the house.

I played with the grasshoppers that hopped in front of me when I would take a step, and I was fascinated by all of the critters that inhabited our yard: the birds, the garter snakes, and the ants moving about the anthills on the sidewalk in our front yard. All creatures great and small held interest for me.

The butterflies that would gracefully flit from flower to flower mesmerized me. I would try to capture them in my hands; however, their elusiveness would leave me empty-handed most times. They were so fragile and beautiful, each one so perfectly given colors and designs that were truly a work of art.

Butterflies became a significant sign for me from that early age. When I was in early grade school, I created a science project demonstrating the life cycle from a caterpillar to a Monarch butterfly. I still have the project because my mom was so great at saving our memorabilia.

This project was not just about the butterfly but also was one of the few times I remember my mom sitting down beside me and helping me with a school project. She helped me draw the butterfly, and to this day, the image of us working side by side is more rewarding than the second place blue ribbon award that I received on the project.

I was born to be a lover of most creatures in nature, except for the *Daddy Long Legs* spiders that my brother used to chase me with! Spending time outside was where I have always been at my happiest. I think I learned very early on and intuitively knew that nature grounded me. If I was feeling sad or upset, plopping down on my stomach in the grass, or climbing up my favorite tree, always brought me peace and comfort.

Being a sibling of a child who dies, regardless of whether we are a child or an adult at the time, is difficult to comprehend with a mixture of emotions swirling around and within each of us.

In talking to many who have experienced the death of a sibling, I have found that we all havemany similar feelings or experiences whether we were born prior to or after the death of our brother or sister. Those feelings can be ones of anger, resentment, abandonment, guilt, and sadness to name a few.

For me, I wasn't sad or angry as a little kid because of Greg's death. How could I be, since I never knew what life was like before his death? I do have questions though, and I wonder, *"Were the days before Greg died happier? Did my family laugh? Did they play? Did they sing? Did they dance?"*

It wasn't until I was older that I realized our family home was what I would call *depressed*. In looking back, I don't remember much laughter, and if you look at pictures of our family from when I was a child, there were not a lot of genuine smiles in those photos.

The only singing in our house was when I was home alone. I would put a record on the stereo and sing with great passion to all of the songs from the *Sound of Music* soundtrack that my parents had in their limited record selection. As I got a little older, I would sneak upstairs and get my oldest brother's Peter, Paul and Mary 's *In the Wind* album from his collection and sing to my heart's content. However, I only did this when I was alone in the house.

I had joy in my heart but it felt like I should not release that joy in the presence of my family, which ultimately resulted in my joy getting buried deep and only coming out on special occasions.

Play is an important way for children to process their emotions. If your child is experiencing grief, encourage them to play. Children can control how their play will "play out," allowing them to learn that they do have control over their feelings and how to deal with them.

Singing is also a great way to release pent up emotions. Music carries a higher vibration than talking, and living at a higher vibration will bring about healing.

Chapter 19

My Best Friend's Death

When I was five years old, three-year-old Joey was my next-door neighbor and my best friend. I still have memories of playing on the little hill that separated our houses, a little hill which seemed gigantic in our eyes. I remember feeling so happy playing with him. The joys of being a child!

I also remember someone telling me that he *died*. I think it was his older sister who told me that he fell out of his bed. I don't know if that is how he died but that image stayed with me for years. I had never fallen out of bed, so I could not grasp why that would happen to him. I am pretty sure I did not know what "dying" meant either.

Years later my mom or someone told me that he had a brain tumor or some medical condition regarding his brain, and I believe his "falling out of bed" had to do with having a seizure. It totally makes sense now, but the five year old me had no clue what it all meant. All I knew at the age of five was one day we were playing and then all of a sudden, he was no longer around. My playmate was gone.

As I got a little older, I would come to know that his little body was laid to rest in a grave close to where my brother Greg was buried. Joey's parents had put a picture of Joey on the gravestone, a picture of him in his little sailor outfit.

That same picture of my little angel friend's face, remains attached to the headstone at his grave to this day. When I go to visit the cemetery, memories of a five year old me with a three year old him playing on the hill, flood back to me as I look at his picture.

As a kid, I would ride my bike and go to the Catholic cemetery, where I would hang out by myself and *visit* my brother Greg, and then I'd walk the few hundred feet off to the right to go *see* Joey. I never felt anxious or uncomfortable at the cemetery. In fact, it was actually quite the opposite. I have always felt at peace and surrounded in comfort knowing that Greg and Joey are right there with me when I go to visit their gravesites.

They say that little children have a greater

ability to sense or "see" spirits who have passed. Some believe that when a young child has an imaginary friend that they talk to, it most likely is a spirit who is seen by the young eyes and believing soul of a child.

I don't recall ever seeing or hearing anyone at the cemetery or during my playtime as a kid. I just *knew* that I wanted to be connected to Greg and to Joey. I believe that I was drawn to the cemetery as a child because that is where I *felt* the strongest connection to those two souls, my brother and my best friend. I believe without a doubt that I have two beautiful spiritual guides in Greg and Joey, walking beside me since I was a little girl.

I am convinced that Greg's spirit came back onto this earth through birth, as a part of me. I alsobelieve Joey came back as a spirit guide to help me achieve my *Life Purpose*, to be a

Mourning's Light, and to bring light to those who grieve.

Going through transitions in life can help us determine our Life Purpose. A Life Purpose is the reason why we are born, and the reason we walk the path and experience the experiences on this earth as we do.

As you will read below, revisiting my childhood and Joey's death has helped me be more compassionate and understanding for those who grieve.

Joey's Mom

The sister of my early childhood friend Joey, recently posted a picture on Facebook for *"siblings' day."* It was a picture of her, in her first communion dress, surrounded by her family. There, sitting in the front, was my *best* friend.

Seeing this picture of him with his family had me thinking back to my childhood, and about his mother, another grieving mom. Joey's mom seemed distant to me, probably similar to how her kids recall how my mother was. I recall seeing Joey's mom come home from work, or sometimes I would see her in the house when I would go over to play with her kids, but I don't remember ever really talking to her or getting to know her.

It resonated with me while writing this book, that Joey's mom was another grieving mom. Another mother whose heart was shattered after her little child died. I thought to myself, *how could one be joyful at a time when your heart is absolutely broken in pieces with sorrow?*

I thought about how different it might have been if my mom and this woman who lived next door had actually talked with each other, connecting at that level of understanding by being two grief-stricken mothers. What if back in the 1950's and 1960's, there were support groups like we have today, similar to Compassionate Friends or Children's Grief Connection?

I was saddened that I had spent my childhood believing Joey's mom and my mom were aloof and un-engaged parents. The truth was that they were two women who would always grieve, women whose homes were filled with other children, and homes that were forever changed the day their children died.

Always flow Love and do not judge if someone is quiet or distant for we do not know his or her stories or their pain.

Chapter 20

Not a Great Fit

Have you ever gone clothes shopping and found something you really liked while it was on the hanger but as soon as you took it to the dressing room, it didn't look or feel right? The size fit, the color was okay, but it just wasn't a *great* fit. That is kind of how I felt growing up.

We had a lot of neighborhood kids on our block but after my buddy Joey died, I felt a bit lost. I didn't really fit in with the kids that were 2 or 3 years older than me. As I got older, I would join in with the neighborhood kids for games like *Kick the Can* and *Tag,* but for the most part, I would play by myself engrossed in the lives of those snakes, bugs, grasshoppers and butterflies.

I also spent a lot of time hanging out in the limbs of the apple trees in our front yard, engulfed in the foliage of the leaves - staying hidden - a place where I could watch what was happening in my surroundings without anyone being able to see me.

It was nice when Vickie moved in across the street. She was my age so we played quite a bit with each other. I recall spending more time at her house than mine, with her mom home all of the time. I liked being in a home where there was activity, noise, oh yeah, and the smell of baking bread! It was so different from our quiet house where most of the time no one was around.

I wasn't a total loner. I had friends in grade school, and I would go to their homes once in a while to play, and I did the usual activities like slumber parties and Girl Scouts. I wouldn't say I was the most popular, but I also wasn't the least popular.

I think I just "was." I had friends but it wasn't like I needed to have a lot of friends. Pretty much like how I am today. I am content with a small group of friends, and I like my alone time to spend time in my own thoughts.

Recently I was talking with one of my friends from grade school about going to each other's homes to play when we were kids. Betsy came from a family of nine kids, and I loved going to her house with all of the commotion and energy. She told me that she loved coming to my house because it was so quiet. She solidly hit that nail on the head - our house was *extremely* quiet!

Isn't that the way we are at times, wishing we had what others have, and their wishing they had what we have?

I also loved going to my grandparent's farm, sometimes bringing a friend with for the weekend, but most of the time I just went out to the farm by myself. I think the farm was a place of peace for me because I was that girl of nature through and through. Let me get my hands dirty, walk dirt roads, and listen to the birds sing in the fields, and I am one happy girl!

I think I liked being alone because I really never felt like I truly belonged in our family.

As a kid with three older brothers, I was told more than a few times that I was adopted. My brothers were pretty convincing by telling me that I was the only one in the family with blond hair, and I was the only girl on dad's side of the family until my cousin, Barb, was adopted into our family when I was three years old.

I remember sneaking into my parents' important papers and combing through documents trying to find my adoption records. I was so sure that I would find evidence that I didn't really belong to this family, evidence that my brothers were right all along.

It wasn't until my mom showed me an article she had written when I was born that I knew that I was birthed into this family. I was just a bit different than the rest with my light-colored hair and being a girl.

"It is unbelievable how much stir one little girl, weight 7 lbs. 8 ½ oz. can make in a family. She arrived Sunday Morning and had completely charmed her father in a matter of minutes. As for me, I'm not the only gal in the family any more, but I like it that way too. Her brothers haven't made her acquaintance as yet, but I'm sure she will win them over in a hurry."

(Excerpt from 1958 article in Shakopee Argus newspaper)

I think it probably was a relief for me to have proof that I wasn't adopted, but I have to be honest, I still did not feel that kinship that I saw other siblings have in other families. I love my brothers but it is a "distant" kind of love. I didn't have a lot of history shared with my oldest brothers so we are not extremely close, and to this day, we still are not a family that I would describe as "close-knit."

If it were not for my mother being the common thread within our family tapestry, I am pretty sure the rest of the threads in our family would be loose, uneven stitches running throughout the fabric.

Recently, my mom said to me: "When I die, none of you will probably ever see each other again," and that might be a fairly accurate insight into what could happen. I do not think our family interaction would cease on purpose, but would most likely be few and far between because we don't have a lot in common, other than being birthed by the same parents.

We are bound by genetics, and genetics do not always create the strongest of bonding material for families.

Shared experiences and time spent with one another is how a family tapestry is woven together.
Purposely choose threads of vibrant and joy-filled colors to tightly weave together the family fabric.

Chapter 21

Lessons in Humanity

I think it is important for me to share a bit of my religious upbringing and how it shaped me to understand how I came to be this light for those who grieve.

As a child, I remember taking an old Bible that my mom had up on the bookshelf in our living room and going into my bedroom at night to read the stories. I loved reading about Jesus, especially how exciting it was when he was born, but I remember how sad I would get when I read about the time of his death. I would literally get a big lump in my throat and hold back tears as I read the story over and over again.

In my Catholic home, we were not taught to read the Bible, but for some reason, it was my book of choice as a little kid in grade school. No one knew what I was doing as I was lying in my bed in my room at night, not my mom, not my dad, not my brothers or my friends. I am not quite sure what they would have thought about this little girl who was so engrossed in the Bible.

As Catholics, we were taught to memorize prayers. In our home, we recited prayers that I had no idea what the words meant. We just did as we were programmed to do. We were expected to behave within a pretty strict set of rules and rituals that we were taught by the priests and nuns.

I didn't follow those rules though. I was the kid who had *conversations* - not memorized prayers - with God all of the time as a child. I was, and still am, a pretty chatty girl in my head, so I would talk to God on a continuous basis. These silent conversations were always very reflective and deep, even as a little kid in grade school.

It was only recently in a conversation with my mom, that I learned not everyone has conversations like that with God. We were sitting on the side of her bed one evening, and I asked her if she ever talked to her friends who have passed away.

Mom looked at me as if I was a bit crazy and

shook her head "*no.*" She told me, "*I say my prayers every night and pray for a long list of people.*"

I then asked her if she ever talked to God throughout the day, and again, she looked at me with a funny look and said "*No!*" Then she looked at me and said, "*I do pray to the Blessed Virgin.*"

I told her that I talk to God, to Angels, to Jesus, Mother Mary, and to my deceased friends and family. I basically will have a conversation with anyone that has died and who happens to pop into my mind.

Mom looked at me and asked me in a very serious and sincere tone of voice: "Do people think you are strange?" I told her that some people might think I am a bit "*whooey*" (as my husband calls it)!

I told her that I am okay if people question who I am and what I say, because I know in my heart that I am surrounded by loved ones whose spirits remain with me, and that I also know that God is way okay with being bombarded by my thoughts and questions!

As I stated earlier, I do not remember a lot of things from my childhood, including anything about kindergarten, absolutely *nothing*. I have family and friends who seem to remember the tiniest of details of their lives as a kid and I sit here with nothing, **NADA**, not one single memory from my kindergarten years.

I have no idea why I don't have memories of what I would imagine would be a significant turning point in my life. I mean, starting school is a big deal – right? Maybe it just was a *non-event* and no big deal for me.

I also have no memories of going to first grade at St. Mary's Catholic school, but boy oh boy, do I remember second grade! Second grade was a very early defining moment in my life. It was the time that **I DIDN'T WEAR MY SNOW BOOTS TO SCHOOL!**

There you have it, my deep dark secret. I didn't wear boots and there was snow on the ground. Heaven forbid! I was punished for not wearing boots to school that day and I had to sit outside the door to the first grade classroom while the rest of the second graders got to go out and play for recess.

I was mortified that I had to sit outside the door of the first grade classroom, like I was the lead character of some shaming ritual, all because my little six-year-old self did not remember to wear boots.

Little did the nuns know that my mom worked full-time, my dad was at the gas station he owned, and my brothers probably did not think about telling me to wear my snow boots that day.

Unfortunately, from that day forward I became a little girl who hated authority. I thought to myself, *"F#*k you, all you nuns and teachers!"* Yes, I was the little kid who learned to use the "F" word early in life, and I became the kid who rolled her eyes and stuck her nose up in the air in a gesture of disdain for the teachers, especially those nuns.

It was easy for me to turn my back on their teachings because there was so much that did not ring true for me. Memorizing prayers without having a clue what they meant didn't make any sense to me. Having to obey the rules of the Church didn't sit well with me when I saw how the teachers treated my classmates or myself when we misbehaved. It definitely was not out of love and kindness.

It was when the nuns who were supposed to be the epitome of goodness publicly shamed me at the age of six where something inside just snapped.

Even though I became a rebellious little thing when it came to the nuns and lay teachers, I continued to have great conversations with the God I knew in my heart, the all loving, all forgiving God who did not judge me, but loved me unconditionally.

I think I learned more about Humanity in school than I did about Reading, Writing, and Arithmetic. School gave me an understanding of the cultural norms of people and relationships, and thisunderstanding would stay with me for the rest of my life.

I specifically remember the time when I was given the old heave-ho out of the clique led by the popular girl in our grade school. I was probably only in third or fourth grade, but I remember it like it was yesterday.

Going to a religious-based school definitely did not teach us kindness or compassion. One would think those attributes would have been the cornerstone of our education, but we were little kids who learned through our interactions with each other what was accepted or not.

I don't recall the girls saying really mean things to each other when we were young, and we definitely did not say things like what I see and hear goes on in schools today. We weren't bullies but we were experts at using the *silent treatment,* the punishment of ignoring the person who was ousted from the clique.

I imagine we learned this particular ostracizing technique from our mothers, the mothers who didn't speak out against their spouses when they were really angry but instead held their feelings inside, close to the vest.

When I drew the short straw and was the target to be exiled from our clique, I remember going to the grocery store with my mom on that Saturday morning. One of my friends from school was there and when I said "hi" to her, she totally ignored me.

That *cold shoulder* routine cut through me like a knife. I was treated as if I was invisible by this girl, and I was devastated. I had no clue why I was no longer a part of the popular group, no clue what I did or did not do, and I have no idea how long I was out of the group nor what it took for me to get back in favor with the group.

I just remember during that period of time, someone was always left out and then they would be brought back into the fold. Someone else was then booted out, a continuous cycle of in and out depending on what the group leader had in mind for that day or week.

I also know that we have experiences in this life in order to learn, and one thing I learned at an early age was that being ignored did not sit well with me. I can see that throughout my life and my career, I have always needed to have a voice and not be ignored. As I have been writing this book, I see that being ignored or not heard can create life-long insecurities and sadness, and it can delay healing from grief.

I think that one incident of being the outcast taught me at a very young age to not exclude others and to try and be a loving person on this earth. When I hear or see evidence of discrimination or divisiveness, I get emotionally upset and that is when my inner anger will surface up front and center!

My heart goes out to the people who have been ousted from their families, friends and society because they live a different lifestyle, and I am not afraid to speak my opinion when it shows up in front of me. In my mind, it is a matter of right and wrong. To me, it is wrong to treat anyone as if they are not as good as someone else.

I remember when I was working as a young nurse taking care of young men with AIDS in the 1980's, when AIDS was new and everyone was scared they would "catch it." I do not recall exactly what precipitated it, but I wrote a passionate *Letter to the Editor* of our local paper, which cried out for compassion to those who were afflicted with AIDS. I had heard too many times where people would say that gay men "deserved" that disease. *Seriously?*

How could anyone who had even the slightest exposure to Christianity, believe that anyone should be ostracized and riddled with a terminal illness because they were different than the masses? Didn't Christ heal the lepers? Didn't Mary Magdalene, a known prostitute, become one who sat at his table?

Yep, I could get pretty whipped up over what I perceived as injustices done to other people.

Chapter 22

A 1960's Life With Dad

I have very fond memories of my dad when I was little. When I would walk into the room, his eyes would just sparkle when he saw me. I knew without any doubt how much he loved me, and he wasn't afraid to show it. As a little girl, he would let me sit on his lap when he came home from work and read the paper while he was having a cocktail. It was a time and place where I felt so protected and loved.

As I got into grade school, he would take me

with him to his friends' homes, and it was awesome when we spent time with his buddy who had a home on the lake. I gained a new friend, Billie, the daughter of dad's friend.

Billie was fun and really nice, letting me hang out and tag along as she went to her horseback riding lessons down the road from their house. We also spent a lot of time swimming in the lake, while our dads sat outside up by the house, telling stories and drinking cocktails into the afternoon.

Interestingly, my mom never went on those outings. It was only just Dad and I.

Dad would also take me to hang out when he went to his friend's home that was a few blocks from our house. The two of them would watch sports on TV, while talking and drinking a cocktail or two. As I think back, I wonder, *why on earth was I brought along to hang out with my dad and his buddies?*

Every so often, Dad would take me out to the lake south of town, for us to throw in our fishing lines from the dock to try and catch sunfish. I recall catching more Bullheads than anything but just spending time with my dad was totally worth trying to remove those scary fish from my hook!

My dad and I were definitely buddies during my early grade school years, but as time went on, our time together became less frequent and he was away from home more and more.

My dad was never violent but he drank, and his drinking and resulting behavior - driving while drinking, spending money he didn't have, and allowing the drinking to affect his work - worsened as my brother Mike and I got older.

I remember the parties where several of my parents' friends would get together for the summer holidays such as Memorial Day, Fourth of July, and Labor Day. They are some of my most enjoyable memories because everyone was having fun, yet looking back, most of the adults would get pretty sloshed and we kids were left to our own devices which was not always a good thing.

As children, we would play with sparklers or fire crackers, run around playing games, or go swimming if we were at someone's cabin on a lake. The air was filled with laughter and the noisy chatter of children playing with total abandon.

The adults would all be sitting around in

chairs, laughing, telling stories and drinking cocktails or beer. Now as I look back, I think to myself, *"Man, they were having one hell of a time partying back then!"*

My mom wasn't one to really join the partying; in fact, she was the "responsible one," the parent who always kept her eye out for the kids to make sure they were safe.

She says she remembers the parties at the lake because she could not swim but she had to watch the kids who were swimming because the rest of the adults were having the time of their lives, visiting, laughing, and drinking while not paying attention to what the children were up to.

As I have been getting reacquainted with some of my old playmates and friends from childhood, I realize that many of our families were a bit screwed up. I have learned that my family wasn't the only family that had its sadness and issues going on behind closed doors. Some of my friends' parents also had messed up marriages and lives.

Extra-marital affairs, physical abuse, verbal abuse, and alcoholism ran rampant within many families. The men of that era seemed to have a lot of issues. I am not sure if it was due to serving in WWII as young men, or for other reasons.

Our mothers either stuck their heads in the sand and pretended things were not out of control in their homes, or they stayed in bad marriages because they needed the financial stability that their husbands provided. It also was an era of keeping the secrets hidden - *don't ask and don't tell.*

As kids, we probably all thought that it was only our own family who had its issues, but now that we are older and open to sharing our "secrets," we know there were many skeletons in the closets of a lot of our homes in our small community.

Chapter 23

Growing Up Without Direction

I was a child in eighth grade, what is called middle school today, with a belligerent attitude and hormones kicking in. I remember being so angry when I got my period. For some reason I thought all of those female changes stopped me from hanging out with my dad.

I wanted to continue our times of going fishing or hanging out at *Raceway Park* watching the cars race around the little track.

I was a tomboy and getting my period meant that life was going to change. I instinctively knew that the relationship with my dad had to change as I grew into a young woman.

My mom grew up in a boarding school so she never talked to me about the changes going on in my body because she had no clue how to talk about those things. No one had taught her when she was young either.

I remember my neighbor, Cheryl, coming to me one day and saying with disgust, "Your mom needs to get you a razor so you can shave your armpits." I looked at her with total confusion, and then I rose up my arm and looked under my armpits. I was horrified! Here I was running around in sleeveless tops with bushels of black, wiry hair growing out of my armpits.

I was frustrated with my mom for not recognizing that I was going through these changes and not doing anything to help me prepare for them.

How could she not let me know what was happening in my body?

It was embarrassing to get my period and having "accidents" because I wasn't prepared. Here I was a girl in a house full of boys, and now I really was different than my brothers. It wasn't all in my head anymore - I didn't fit in!

By the time I hit seventh and eighth grade, I had zero tolerance for authority. I did not apply myself at all to school because that would be complying with what "they" wanted, and I would have nothing to do with that! My report cards reflected my attitude so I would bring them to my dad to sign so my mom would not see them.

I was afraid of my mom's reaction when I got in trouble, not because she raised her voice or her hand to me. I was afraid I would get the *cold shoulder* from her, that she would silently go around the house and pretend I wasn't there, because that is how she handled her anger and frustrations.

I look upon my mom now with sadness for her and what life must have been like when I was an obnoxious pre-teen. She was grieving the death of her child and most likely the death of her marriage, and here I was, totally out of control and she had no one to help her reign me in.

My dad never paid any attention to my mom except when he would bring her a gift bought at the local dress shop. He always remembered the special occasions by buying her a gift of clothing, but he never reached out to comfort or support her physically or emotionally.

Dad just went off into his own life, surrounding himself with his buddies at the bar, drowning whatever his sorrows were in alcohol, and leaving my mom to grieve in silence while raising four children who were in various stages of life.

My brothers could have used a healthy, strong male figure to teach them how to be disciplined in ways that may have helped them avoid some of the unpleasant consequences of their actions, while they were teenagers and young adults.

My older brothers were teenagers and young

adults of the sixties, the era of drugs, sex, and rock and roll and I wanted to be just like them. I wanted to be a child of the sixties!

I remember my oldest brother leaving home. Steve went into the Marine Corp during the Viet Nam war, and he was shipped off to Okinawa, a place I had never heard of. At my young age, I didn't understand the impact of the war like we do in this day and age of an overabundance of media coverage.

I cannot imagine how frightened my mother must have been to have her oldest child go off to a foreign land where he could possibly be in harm's way. Losing one child is horrible; to possibly lose another to war is unimaginable, and my mom was a worrier, always worrying and fearing what bad thing might happen.

My brother Dave also went away and joined

the Army. I remember him coming home on leave when my mom was really sick and hospitalized from a ruptured ovary. I was only twelve, and the events surrounding that time are imprinted on my mind forever.

Mom was deathly ill and had no way to go to the doctor. Dad was nowhere to be found. Dave was home with an army buddy, doing what young guys did when they were home on leave, partying.

Finally a neighbor took my mom into the doctor where she ended up having emergency surgery. She could have easily died from the severity of her condition at that time. She was so sick, and I remember when I went to the hospital to see her, it frightened me to the core.

My mom was so weak and barely able to

talk, not the "in control" mother that I had always known. It was probably the scariest moment of my life up to that point. The woman who was our stability, our rock, was not as strong as I had always imagined her to be.

As I look back on the events of that time, I think that was probably when the marriage between my parents pretty well disintegrated.

My mom could not trust my dad to be around if she needed him, and she did not trust his judgment due to how he handled a situation with my brother, Dave, at that time, which ended badly. I am not going to go into any detail but suffice it to say, the silence around our home became even more deafening as the marriage of my parents crumbled around us.

When living in grief, it is hard for the parents to pay attention to their children, and the kids may be left on their own to figure out life. Sometimes it does take "a village to raise a child." Take the time to gently provide direction and support to the children of your village when you see them veering off the right path.

‘

Chapter 24

Go Ask Alice

Do you remember the 1971 book, *Go Ask Alice*, which was turned into a movie in 1973? It is a fictitious "diary" of a teenager who started a downward slide into the world of drugs. When I first saw the movie back in the early 70's, it resonated with me. I could have been the lead character in the movie.

I was probably twelve, going on thirteen when I smoked my first cigarette. I was also thirteen when I smoked my first joint. By the time I was fourteen, I unknowingly did my first hit of acid. I liked hanging around with the older crowd, and I had been at some guy's house with a bunch of other people when I was given the acid. I had no clue what it was or what it would do, but I didn't think anything of taking drugs and the potential effect if might have on me.

I had come home from a dance at the local Knights of Columbus Hall and I remember lying in bed, hallucinating like crazy, totally out of control in my head. I started to scream and quickly got out of bed and went into the kitchen.

My mom came running out from her bedroom to see what was going on with me, which straightened me up immediately! I quickly came up with the story that I had just woken myself up from a bad dream. I am not sure if she really bought my lame story, but after a few minutes of checking me over, she finally let me go back to bed.

My mom has always been pretty intuitive and I am a horrible liar, so I am sure she knew something was not right, but how would she have any clue I was tripping on acid? My mother was pretty naïve when it came to the whole drug scene.

I remember my brother Mike came running down the stairs from his bedroom that night, and I could tell that he knew what was up. He gave me a look that I remember to this day, a look of disgust. Yep, he knew, I could see it in his eyes.

I loved hanging out with the older crowd, especially the guys. The whole need to be a part of a group, to be included, to be seen and heard, and this need for acceptance took me down a path that I followed for several years.

I don't know how I got away with smoking and partying at such a young age. *Was no one home watching over us?* I remember going to keg parties out in the country and the cops coming to break up the parties. *How the heck did I get away with it? How did I get to run around town with no controls? Where were my parents?*

Even during my *Wild Child* period, I still would go spend time with my grandmother who had moved into town after selling the farm. For some reason, I always felt secure in my relationship with Grandma Schmitt and I would never think of acting out in front of her or treating her with disrespect. In fact, all of my grandparents garnered a great deal of respect from me. I honored all of them for being the patriarchs and matriarchs of our family.

As I think about our family dynamics, I find it interesting that my grandmother could not give her own daughter, my mom, the feelings of acceptance and security, but she was able to give them to my brother Mike and I. For some reason, we were able to bring out the softness in her heart that she could not show her own daughters.

My freshman year in high school was spent running around doing a lot of things I should not have been doing, such as stealing cigarettes from my dad's carton of King Chesterfields, going to teen dances when I was barely a teenager, smoking pot, and hanging out with guys much older than me. It was a wild time for a very young girl, a young girl who always had an old soul.

I didn't like being home. The atmosphere was unpleasant at best. My dad's absences and alcoholism was taking its toll on everyone. He owed money and took out loans that my mom was not aware of and nothing was worse for my mother than being in debt. She was mortified and very angry when she found out that Dad had debt that he had never discussed with her.

Mom's view on money resulted from being a little child during the depression. She always had a great fear about having a lack of money, whereas my dad was totally carefree about his finances. I know Dad would hide his debt from my mom out of fear. He knew she would be angry and go into her silent treatment mode of existence.

Imagined fear seemed to reign within our home.

Because my mom became a master at performing the silent treatment, she could easily make you become invisible to her if she was angry. I think my dad hated to be made invisible as much as I did, so he hid his money issues and his drinking - classic signs of an addiction out of control.

I remember one particular incident when I was still pretty young, when my parents came home from being out in the evening, most likely to a cocktail party with their friends, and I heard them arguing in the hallway outside of my bedroom.

My mom actually raised her voice to my dad, and then I heard a loud **BANG** on the bathroom door. I sat up in my bed and screamed. I think the shock of my mom actually raising her voice in anger coupled with the bang on the door freaked me out because it was so out of character for my well-controlled and very silent mother.

My brother Steve was at home at that time, maybe he was still in high school, and he came running down the steps, hollering at my parents and telling them to *"f&*king knock it off."*

My big brother, who never raised his voice, came running to the rescue, where he had to take on the role of the adult in our home that night. I remember that someone, not sure if it was my mom or Steve, was hollering at my dad, *"Look at what you did to her!"* Referencing my hysterical crying from thinking my world was falling apart.

As I think back to that night of forty-five years ago or more, I remember my mom coming into my room after all of the commotion had settled down. She came in to check on me, gently stroking my hair, asking me if I was okay. That was the second and last time that I recall my mom coming to comfort me as a child.

It literally took me screaming at the top of my lungs for my parents to break their bubble of anger and sadness so that they could comfort their child.

I want to make it very clear that I do not blame my mom and dad. It just makes me sad that they were in their own hell at the time. My mother was married to an alcoholic and life for her was out of control.

I understand what my mom's life was like being married to my dad, because I chose the same path as a young adult. I married a man who was a serious alcoholic. I did the typical thing many adult children of alcoholics do; I recreated the same scenario in my adult life, somehow thinking that I could make a difference this time around.

My mom has always been a beautiful and caring woman, so I know without a doubt that she wanted to reach out to me so many times in my childhood but she just couldn't. She did not know how to thaw the frozen shield of protection that had formed around her heart, frozen with the icy grips of grief and sadness. Her arms remained firmly at her sides, as her hands were clenched in anger and guilt, living a life filled with unhappiness.

When I was fifteen, my mom's job was being relocated to a small town that was a three-hour drive from our home. It was a small town with a population of twenty-five hundred people. She had decided to wait until my brother, Mike, graduated from high school before moving away.

I remember sitting on the front steps of my childhood home, sobbing my eyes out the day they were packing up our belongings. I cried because I was leaving my home, my family, and my friends. My world, as I knew it, was falling apart. Our family disintegrated until there were only two of us left, my mom and me.

And I was so very angry.

As we were ready to leave town the day we moved, I remember mom taking me to my dad's office where he worked as a realtor, so that I could say goodbye to him.

Seriously, my dad couldn't stay home that day to say goodbye?

I suppose it was just too painful for my dad to be at home and watch the moving truck take away the belongings accumulated after twenty-five years of marriage. I am sure that he could not bear the thought of seeing his wife and daughter leave for the final time.

When I got back in the car after giving my dad a hug goodbye at his office, I buried my head into the little dog I held on my lap and literally sobbed for miles and miles into his furry coat, until there were no tears left. The rest of the ride to our new home was done in complete silence.

I cannot imagine how hard it must have been for my mom to watch her child sob with such grief and know that there was nothing she could do to make it better, because she was in her own world of hurt.

It only took me a matter of a day or two to meet two young girls who were riding around in a truck with some of their guy friends from highschool. They happened to stop after seeing me in the yard of our new home and took me under their wings. Julie and Paula must have known that I was a broken little girl, and I needed a family.

We were the kids from broken or dysfunctional homes. We created our own little family, where we were all accepted and felt loved. We also drowned out our pain by self-medicating with pills, pot and alcohol. Not a great mix for sixteen and seventeen year old children.

Sex, Drugs, and Rock and Roll was more than a slogan in those days. It truly was a way of life. We were seeking acceptance and looking for love. We just did not know how to go about finding it in a healthy way. We did not have the role models who could help us figure out a better path, so we all stumbled our way through those teen-age years, some of us faring better than others.

We would go to school only enough to pass our classes. Thankfully, my mom taught all of her children one very important thing - to have a high work ethic. That high work ethic had me working two jobs after school and on weekends. Unfortunately, my high work ethic at that time was all for the sake to make enough money to buy the bags of pot, speed, and alcohol that were consumed throughout my years in high school.

I have to say that I honestly have a lot of fun memories of my high school years and I do not really hold great regret for that time. However, there are also those memories where I think, *"oh my God, how could I have done that...?"*

Six months before my class's graduation, I had already accrued all of the credits required to graduate by taking all of the English classes offered by our little high school. I find it pretty amazing that I was able to accomplish getting all of my credits **and** be an *honor graduate* all while spending the majority of my days and nights partying with my friends.

I believe that my ability to never veer totally off course was due to the fact that I have always had an inner guide, my brother Greg. I also know that little Joey stayed close to me as my spirit guide, helping to keep me on a path that would someday bring me to the life I was meant to live.

It would have been so easy for me to walk

down a path of total self-destruction while under the influence of drugs or alcohol, but I always had this inner compass, which lit up like a beacon, flashing in my face to get my attention when I was coming upon crossroads during my teenage years.

I could have easily taken the needle when I was watching people shoot up drugs into their veins, but I didn't. I could have easily run away for parts unknown, but I didn't. I could have easily died from alcohol poisoning when I consumed the two half pints of Peppermint Schnapps at the age of sixteen, but I didn't.

I watched people take the drug Quaalude where they would appear to be literally melting into the pavement because they could not stand on their own two feet. I could have done the same, but I didn't.

There were also times, when I did take chances and it was during one of those times where I called upon God to help me through.

One night I took some "blotter acid" with a girlfriend when we were in high school. We were up in her bedroom and decided to take a little more than what we were told to take because we weren't feeling any effects. It didn't take long before we were both hallucinating like crazy, and the trip just kept going from bad to worse, as we left her house and the watchful eyes of her parents, to go "uptown" and hang out with our friends at the local bar. Yes, at sixteen, we would hang out in the bar with our older friends.

I finally got myself home that evening after hiding out for who knows how long in the darkened movie theatre that was next to the bar, trying to talk myself down. As I lay in bed that night, I was too scared to close my eyes.

I kept thinking about the stories of people doing crazy stuff on acid and I was paranoid that if I closed my eyes, I would lose total control of my sanity and be one of those people who did something stupid, like jumping out of the second story window. I remember praying to God and telling him *"If you make sure I come out of this night alive, I promise I will NEVER, EVER, take acid again!"*

I put my faith in God and my prayers were answered. I also kept my promise and that was the last time I would ever take acid again in my life.

I was destined to live and experience many of life's dualities in order to come fully into the person I am today, to be that light for those who grieve.

I had to experience fear, in order to understand true faith. I had to experience grief, in order to understand compassion. I had to experience anger, in order to understand forgiveness. I had to experience chaos many times in my life, in order to learn true peace.

I decided to go to college at the age of seventeen when I had gotten all of my high school credits. That decision was made after my mother gave me an ultimatum – either I go to college or find a full-time job because she wasn't going to let me *sit around and just smoke pot with my friends all day,* as she so eloquently put it! I started college during the winter semester, when the rest of the kids were already acclimated and into the rhythm of college life.

It was when I moved away to go to college

that first time when life again changed for me. I found that I could no longer smoke pot without getting extremely paranoid, and I didn't drink because I was not old enough. Since the college was one hundred miles away and I did not drive, I would stay in the dorm and study on most weekends when I did not find a ride to go home.

The other kids from college were hitting the bars on weekends because the drinking age was eighteen. Since I was only seventeen, I once again had the feeling that I did not fit in. I was away from my friends and lost in a sea of unfamiliar faces, attending college classes where I felt insecure and not very intelligent.

Over the next couple of years, I went to college but really was not *involved*. I had no idea what I really wanted to do with my life and I frankly never gave it much thought. I was just going through the motions of life, but not really living fully.

Chapter 25

A Healer Begins to Emerge

It was during the summer break from college in 1976, when my mom told me that I had an opportunity to work at the local nursing home for the summer, so I went to work in the housekeeping department. I remember how it seemed like all I did was mop floors, which is pretty much what I did. Imagine eight hours a day of mopping floors; it was boring beyond belief!

Then I was asked to be a nursing assistant. I

have no clue how I went from housekeeping to being a nursing assistant, but I imagine there was a bit of divine intervention in that decision because it ultimately changed the course of direction in my life.

I remember the nun who was in charge of the nursing home. She was a short, stocky woman who intimidated the heck out of me. If she told me to go be a nursing assistant, I figured I had better do what she said, or there would be consequences that I would not want to have to deal with!

I remember the day when a red-headed older and seasoned nursing assistant took me into a room, filled a basin of water and put it on the bedside table with a bar of soap, a washcloth and a towel. She told me I needed to give the resident a bath, and then she turned around and walked out the door of the room, leaving me all alone with a young guy who was in his mid twenties!

Doug was paralyzed with no movement of his legs and had only gross motor movements of his upper arms. The look of fear on my face must have been lit up like marquee lights! *Holy Crap! I am supposed to give this guy a bed bath?*

I was mortified and stood there like a statue, not saying a word, frozen in terror! Then Doug said to me, *"What are you so embarrassed about? I should be the one who is embarrassed, laying here and having to have you give me a bath! Pick up the washrag and I will tell you what you need to do."*

That was my first time caring for another human being who was totally dependent on me to take care of his needs. That was the defining moment that gave me a clear vision for my future – I wanted to become a nurse.

As I think back on that time, I realize that Doug was probably one of the most influential people in my life. He was a humble and caring teacher; not only for me, but also for the many young people who came into his room to help him with his self cares. Many young people left his room and pursued careers in the medical field.

Doug took the time and had the patience to make us all feel like we could really make a difference, that we were good and caring people. It is pretty clear to me that Doug was put on this earth to teach others humility and compassion.

When he dove into the water as a teenager, hitting his head and severing his spinal cord, he started his true journey on this earth. He became paralyzed so he could be a teacher to every person who entered his room at the nursing homes where he resided. Doug was a true Earthly Angel who took his soul contract seriously, seriously enough to give up ever being able to walk in this life so that he could teach and encourage others.

My experiences working as a nursing assistant started me on a path to become a nurse. I enjoyed caring for those who could not take care of themselves, especially our elderly.

I still partied a bit through college and nursing school, but as I matured in age, I also matured in behavior. I was on my path as a healer, finding a purpose for my life. I didn't need to self-medicate anymore because I found that if I gave to others, I felt good about myself.

When we give from the heart to help others, we will find healing for ourselves. As we give, we will receive light and love flowing back into our hearts.

Chapter 26

Learning To Forgive

After I graduated from nursing school, I moved to a town in northern Minnesota up by the Canadian border. I moved there because there were not a lot of nursing jobs in the state, so I had to go where I could find work.

Many people think of me as an extreme extrovert because when I am with groups of people, I gather energy from those around me. However, there is also that shy little girl who resides within me from my days as a toddler – that shy little girl who is still a bit insecure and not sure how to go about making friends.

Moving to Thief River Falls was a big decision for me because I did not know a soul in that town, and it meant that I would be two hours away from my mom and friends from high school. Moving to a town far away from my family and friends, where I did not know anyone, ended up being a really good thing for me because I became independent and paid my own bills. I was proud to be self-sufficient, and proud that I had created this life for myself.

Then I met Bill – a funny, seemingly happy guy, with a great sense of humor that would emerge from the mischievous little boy from within. We ended up living together on weekends because he was gone on the road during the week, working as a roofer.

We got married in 1985. Up until that point, I had never entertained the thought of getting married. Living with parents who had a loveless marriage left me with the perception that marriage was not my idea of living a fulfilling life.

As a teenager, I used to dream of having ten acres in the country, a trailer house, and a horse. I didn't dream of anything fancy, and I definitely **did not** dream about having a husband, but for some reason, I changed my mind. I decided it was time to settle down just like all my friends were doing, so we got married.

We moved back to my original hometown where my dad and one of my brothers lived. I got a job as a nurse, and Bill worked construction, initially with my brother, and then moving to a company that did commercial construction.

We did not have a lot of friends, and I didn't like going out with him because he tended to get drunk easily, which would embarrass and anger me.

Sounds like a familiar scene from my childhood.

We eventually stopped going out at all, and about six months into the marriage, I became pregnant.

I remember when I found out I was pregnant, I was afraid to tell my mother. At a time when I should have been ecstatic with this little life growing inside of me, I was fearful of my mom's reaction. How weird is that?

I think I was afraid that she would not be happy about my news. Interestingly enough, my mother reacted in a way that I had feared, with no excitement, no congratulations, nothing.

As I mentioned earlier, my mother is pretty intuitive, so maybe she wasn't excited about my pregnancy because she sensed that my marriage was already in trouble. Or perhaps she was not thrilled beyond belief because of fear for what could go wrong in having a child.

When I was about three months pregnant, Bill was injured in a work-related accident, falling twenty-five feet to the ground from some beams he was tying in on a building construction job. He sustained a significant fracture to his leg, which required him to be in a hard leg cast that covered his foot and went up to his upper leg. It took over two years of being casted and having a surgery to finally heal.

Unfortunately, Bill was an alcoholic, and his alcoholism ran rampant quickly as he recovered from the work injury. We went through four treatment programs (two of them in-patient), during a two-year period of time. I was attending Al Anon, working full-time, and taking care of our child when I wasn't working. The marriage ended when it was clear that sobriety was not how Bill chose to live his life.

I was a single parent with a very angry little four-year-old boy. Turnabout is fair play – right? I was the angry little girl pretty much abandoned emotionally by my dad, and it was my mom who had made the decision to end the marriage. I created the exact same story for my child.

Human behavior is fascinating. My husband had alcoholism just like his dad, and he hated growing up in that environment, yet he followed the same path. I hated growing up with a dad who was an alcoholic and parents who could not stand to live in the same house with each other, and yet I created the same scenario.

I realize now that I created the same story in my life because my life path required me to experience what my mom experienced as a wife and a mother. If I had not lived a similar story, I am not sure that I would have been able to find the forgiveness I needed to give to both of my parents for those younger years when I felt betrayed and abandoned by the two people I depended on the most.

I also needed to walk this path in order to learn true forgiveness. Bill came into my life as another soul contract, a contract that gave me the learning experience to forgive him and myself.

I also was able to teach my child the impact forgiveness can have when given freely to another, with no strings attached. After a decade of abandonment, my son reached out to his dad to forgive him. He gave his dad the gift of forgiveness with perfect timing. Six months later, his dad died unexpectedly. Bill was able to transition from this earth with a free heart filled with love from his child.

Chapter 27

Judge Not

As a young woman in my twenties, I was comfortable being around those who were transitioning from life to death. Maybe it was why I came onto this earth and was born into a grieving family.

My cousin Rick and I were the same age. We played together as small children in the sandbox, and we went through school together until my mom and I had moved away when I was fifteen.

Rick and I were friends more than being relatives. We always had a connection, and that never went away after I moved to another city to attend high school. We stayed loosely connected, and we saw each other during family events such as weddings.

When we were in our twenties, Rick developed a brain tumor, one so serious that it resulted in several years of chemotherapy. Rick had gotten married, and the stress of his illness ultimately led to the demise of his marriage. He eventually moved back home to live with his parents as he fought for his life.

This was the same time that my then-husband and I had moved back to my hometown, giving Rick and I a chance to reconnect. I remember going to see him for the first time after he had been through a few years of chemotherapy, and I was shocked to see the skeleton of his former self, sitting in the chair. Yes, his body was deteriorated but his sense of humor and devilish glint in his eye was still there. The body was weak, but his soul was still very much intact!

When Rick was in his final days of transition from this life, he was a patient on the Oncology ward of the hospital where I worked. I worked the night shift as a nurse on the medical/surgical unit a few floors up from his room.

I spent time with Rick whenever I could while he was in the hospital, even though he could no longer communicate and Grand Mal seizures were coming one right on top of the other. I made sure that he was given the medication to calm down the seizure activity before his parents would come to visit. I could not let my aunt and uncle see their child in continuous seizure activity, where the spasms were so great that they would literally shake the whole bed .

The night I intuitively knew he was in his transition phase of death, I left my floor and came to sit with him. I called my aunt and uncle letting them know that I did not believe Rick would make it through the night, and they told me that they just could not come. They could not bear to see their child die.

I held Rick's hand that night and talked softly to him, letting him know that I was with him, and that it was okay for him to leave this earth. He had fought a valiant fight, and it was now time to go where he could be at total peace. I told him how much his parents loved him.

My aunt and uncle were so grateful that I

was with Rick when he passed, but at that time, I had difficulty comprehending how they could not be with their child and hold his hand, to have their voices be the last voices he heard on this earth.

It wasn't until recently, when I was a volunteer at the family grief camp, where I really understood why my aunt and uncle could not be at the hospital that night. I finally "felt" within the depths of my being, how excruciating that decision that was for my aunt and uncle.

It took a weekend in the company of some grieving parents to understand the absolute raw pain that my parents and my aunt and uncle had experienced. The death of a child has got to be the most difficult experience any human being can go through.

There is no right or wrong way to "be" around the death of a child. As observers to this grieving process, let us not judge how parents react, but hold them in love.

Chapter 28

A Marriage Contract

After my divorce, the last thing I could imagine was getting married again, and then I met Ken. It was an attraction from the minute we first met, and I finally understood what people meant when they say their partner is their *Soul Mate*.

I recently read a book called, *The Little Soul and the Sun* by Neale Donald Walsch. It is a great children's story that teaches how and why *Soul Contracts* are created.

Basically the story is about a "Little Soul" who resides in Heaven. The Little Soul is having a grand conversation with God about wanting to "be who it was." God talked about having to see the opposite of something to really understand and "be." For example, in order to truly be "One Who Forgives," the Little Soul would need to have an experience, which would create anger or upset in order to understand and learn to forgive.

A "Friendly Soul" came to join the conversation with God and the Little Soul and offered to help the Little Soul experience the negative actions on learning how to forgive.

That is what a *Soul Contract* is; a contract between two souls to help each other learn how to forgive, to love, and to be patient.

I know now, without a doubt, that Ken and I

also created a soul contract long before we came to this life, and it was one doozy of a contract, as you will see!

Three weeks into our marriage, Ken had a massive stroke at the age of thirty-two. I woke up in the middle of the night because his legs were jerking uncontrollably as he laid beside me. When I asked him what was going on, his speech was high pitched and I knew immediately that he had a stroke or some other acute neurological problem.

He lay in a local small town hospital for two days as they tried to get his blood pressure under control, but nothing was working. I demanded to see the on-call physician in the middle of the second night, and we agreed that he needed to go to a different hospital where a specialist could evaluate him.

The next morning, the original treating doctor basically told me that my husband would probably "not make it." I remember driving and silently praying that Ken would survive the ambulance ride to the hospital that was located 100 miles away. I was in a daze, not knowing if my husband would be dead or alive when I finally got to see him again.

When I entered the hospital and met Ken's neurologist in the hallway, I asked him, *"What are his chances?"* The doctor looked at me with a funny look on his face and said, *"What do you mean? He is going to be just fine and should fully recover."*

Once again, God didn't fail me and my prayers were answered. Within three months of therapy to learn how to walk, Ken was recovered enough to ease back into work on a part-time basis.

Approximately twelve or thirteen years ago, Ken was on the brink of death once again and *Nancy Nurse* here had no clue, but I do vividly remember the fight we had the night he almost died.

I was really angry with him because he was putting on massive amounts of weight, and he would fall asleep all of the time without warning. It was Christmas time, and he would sit down and within minutes fall asleep. Christmas Eve was miserable, and I was at my wit's end because it felt like he was totally out of control with his weight and didn't care.

The night I finally "got it" was when I blew up at him, and as I went into the bedroom to give him another dose of my anger, he was packing a bag. I asked him what he was doing and he looked at me and said, "I am going to go stay at a motel."

I suddenly looked into his eyes while the fog of anger lifted, and I really *saw* him. I could see that he was sick. He finally shared what his symptoms were, and I knew he needed to go to the emergency room right away.

Here was my husband, literally dying before my eyes as his oxygen level dropped and his carbon dioxide levels were poisoning him. When we got him to the emergency room that night, the doctors told me he probably would have died within the hour if I had not gotten him to the hospital when I did.

He was diagnosed with a severe case of sleep apnea after a frightening seven-day stint in the Intensive Care Unit (ICU). I had gone to visit him one day, and he was delirious. I finally questioned the nurses and found out that they had given him a sedative the night before, a sedative that could not be metabolized because his organs were shutting down.

I remember that day like it was yesterday. I went home for a break that afternoon and fell to my knees, sobbing and crying out to God. I was so scared that Ken was going to die. I prayed and cried, and prayed some more. After an hour, I got myself up from the floor, washed my face and went back to the hospital.

During that hour that I laid on the floor crying out to God for help, Ken had started coming out of his delirium.

Yep, my prayers were answered once again.

Off Ken went for another ambulance ride, which took him to another hospital where an amazing pulmonary specialist used her intuition to finally diagnose his condition. Once she figured out what was wrong, he received the appropriate treatment and recovered quickly.

As would be our pattern, there was one other time when we were angry at each other, and it took another health scare to turn our thoughts around. Only this time it was me who was the one who landed in the hospital.

I had woken up that morning at 5:00 a.m. with a terrific pain in my chest. It felt like I had pulled a muscle or that something was "caught" in my upper chest. I thought I would just let it be to see if I could work out the pain because it really only hurt when I took a deep breath.

The pain continued throughout the day. It was after I took my dog for a two mile walk that I decided to drive myself to the emergency room, because I did not think I could fall asleep with the pain I was having in my chest.

Since Ken and I were mad at each other for some reason that was probably really benign and/or stupid, I told him I was going to take myself to the emergency room, and off I went, leaving Ken and our puppy at the house.

It didn't take long before Ken was being ushered in my little room in the ER. He made it just in time as I was being wheeled off for an ultrasound of my chest. After the results came back, it was confirmed that I had what looked like a small pulmonary embolism (PE) in each lung.

I remember the look on the doctor's and Ken's faces. They were scared because PEs can be life threatening. Approximately one third of the people who suffer from one will die.

Even though I am a Registered Nurse, I didn't understand what all the fuss was about. Ken and the doctor looked almost sad. It just didn't make sense to me because I felt great after I had an injection for pain! I was even joking around to them that the only time I had pain was when I breathed, so I just *"needed to stop breathing."* No one thought my sense of humor was funny.

I was immediately taken off hormone replacement therapy, which can cause blood clots, and given treatment. To this day, I am not sure if there really were embolisms in my lungs because I have gotten different opinions from doctors, but I do know that health scare, once again gave Ken and I a "wake up" call in our relationship.

As I look back, I have come to believe Ken and I were destined to have these experiences where we had to *move through* the negative energy that was clouding our vision, in order to see the real health issues we were facing. It took these big health scares to remember how much we really did love each other.

Ken and I were put into each other's lives to learn how to honestly love each other during the good times, the ugly times, the happy times, and the sad times.

Yes, Ken's soul contract with me was to teach me how to be "One Who Loves."

I am thankful that we had gone through those times of trials and tribulations before I had those two epiphanies that changed my life significantly these past couple of years. I am sure it has been a bit unnerving for Ken to see his wife change so dramatically in such a short period of time.

I was one who never went out socially, didn't go to church regularly, and pretty much devoted myself to my corporate career. After my epiphanies, I started going to yoga, joined a women's circle and learned how to talk to my Angels. I went on a retreat with a group of ladies I had never met, I started learning about astrology, numerology, and I had readings with intuitive women and psychics.

I also started getting re-acquainted with women from my grade school years, and I have been able to listen and *hold* their stories of grief so that they could find some healing and happiness.

I needed to allow Ken to go through his own processing of what my change meant for him and for us. At first, he didn't want to talk about any of my beliefs or feelings, but now, he supports me fully even if he doesn't understand or totally embraces my beliefs.

I know he is with me on this journey for the long run. He is my rock, my comfort, and the strength that I have been looking for my whole life. I know he will never abandon me physically or emotionally, and he will make sure I am okay.

It is funny that many people have come to me and told me how *great* I am, how *kind* I am, how *supportive* I am, many with no clue about what was going on behind closed doors for many years of my life.

I have not always been the kindest, the most supportive, or the greatest at flowing love to others. It has taken all of these life experiences to help me understand and seek to be a better person in this life.

I think it was important for me to share my whole story for understanding how being born into a grieving family after the loss of a loved one can impact the lives of the children who remain. My hope is that my story will help families make conscious choices on how to deal with the grieving process in healthy ways, so that a child doesn't feel the need to look at unhealthy or dysfunctional ways to feel loved and comforted.

Part III

The Healing Begins

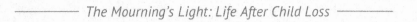

Chapter 29

Scratching the Surface of Grief

It was after the second epiphany a couple of years ago, coming home from the grief camp, when my mother and I began to go *deep* into her grief.

I came home that afternoon and sat with her at our kitchen table and she asked me how camp was. I looked over at her and the tears began again. I told her that after watching those grieving parents all weekend, I could feel her pain. I felt like I truly understood what she and Dad had gone through after Greg's death.

My poor mother, grieving for over sixty years, now had the opportunity to finally be able to open up and share, to finally be honest about how she has felt for so many years. I told her that I thought we needed to write a book about Greg, a book that could help other grieving parents, and that was the genesis of this book.

Over the course of writing this book, my mother and I have had some incredibly powerful conversations that occurred spontaneously. Sometimes, just while we sat watching TV, a conversation about Greg would start out of nowhere. Other times, I asked her questions, and she would share those most painful times of her life.

Since my mom had moved in with our family a few months prior to the decision to write the book, it took us some time to find that small manila envelope that was put away with her important papers. When we located it, together we opened it up and gazed upon the photos of the tiny baby photographed at the mortuary. Only this time, we looked at Greg very differently than we had in the past.

I looked at Greg's pictures with a deep knowing that he is here, within me, as he always has been. My mom looked at Greg's picture with love and sadness in her eyes. She gently moved her finger along his little legs in the picture and said, "*He was just a little baby.*" Oh, how my heart ached to hear this ninety year-old tiny, little lady with such a sad voice.

As she touched the photo some more, she

commented, *"His clothes were too big for him,"* and she gently stroked her finger over his picture a little more. Little baby Greg dressed in an outfit ironed to perfection, with little chubby legs and feet covered in soft white baby slippers, his little arms laying open with his tiny little fingers slightly bent.

Since that day, I carried his pictures throughout the journey of writing our story, bringing him out from that place of hiding and allowing his spirit to be free, free so he could help me write the words that desperately needed to be spoken.

I thought at that time that I wanted his picture to be on the cover of this book, a portrait that would create life in his features. When I started thinking about having this portrait drawn, a young girl immediately came to mind to be the artist.

A young girl I knew who would honor and take great care in creating Greg's image with love. A young girl who just happened to have *Autism,* which is a significant fact that you will come to understand as yet another synchronicity, which occurred as we travelled down the path of writing this story.

I knew that I wanted Greg to be drawn as if he were alive, because it was so important for me to give life to my brother's spirit: The spirit that resides within my heart and my soul. Interestingly, when I told Mom that I was commissioning this young girl to draw Greg's picture, she had one simple request. *"Could you please have her make him look like he is alive?"*

As Mom and I picked away at the scabs of grief, the emotions overflowed. The emotions of sadness and guilt because she never got to hold him after she left the hospital to go home the night he died. The emotion of anger towards the nuns running the hospital for not covering up his tiny body with at least a blanket, and for leaving him out in the hallway all by himself.

Mom and I delved into the questions that plagued her for years... *How long was he lying lifeless before someone at the hospital found him? Why were his little arms already frozen into position? Why did they list his death as pneumonia when he was fine earlier in the day before he went in for his baby shots?*

There were times, as Mom and I talked, when she could tell her story without much emotion. Other times, however, her eyes would stare off into the distance as she talked, and I could tell she had travelled back in time - back to 1952, reliving that exact period of time when her baby boy fell ill and died.

Grief is an extremely powerful emotion which ebbs and flow like the waves in the ocean. Sometimes it gently rolls to and fro, licking at the surfaces of the mind... manageable... other times, the waves erupt out of the dark, angry waters... hurtling against the hard rocks of reality with a forceful vengeance.

Chapter 30

Greg's Spirit Comes Alive

The many months of this writing project have brought some incredible synchronicities throughout my life and the people I have connected with. When I started to share with others that I was writing this book, I was given many affirmations to let me know that this story was an important story to share.

On November 2, 2014, I went to a *Women's Circle* and had a reading by a woman named Cynthia.

Interestingly, Cynthia had done my "soul painting" without knowing anything about me. Along with the "painting" she had written out a note that she had "channeled" for my reading with her.

The note stated, "*I am the Comforter. As I discover the sweetness of comfort offered by The Divine, my heart is filled with softness and light. I rest in the assurance that all is well and certainty of this Truth compels me to radiate Love and Truth to all creatures.*"

It is true, I have been a "Comforter" for those who grieve my entire life, but I never really realized that it was my calling until I started this journey with my mom.

On December 8, 2014, I went to another *Women's Circle* at my yoga instructor's home where I had another reading done, this time by a woman named Heather, who read my astrological charts. This was the first time I had any experience with astrology, so I was a bit skeptical about the information that I would receive from my "reading".

Heather told me that evening, that *"there was a loss in my family before I was born."* She said that it appeared that I had been healing from grief in a previous life, and when I was born into this life, I was born into a grieving family with the purpose *"to heal that grief."*

I believe my journey of understanding my role as a *Comforter* and *providing a light for those who mourn*, started in June of 2012, the month and year that Greg would have turned sixty years old. It was at that time when Mom opened up and talked extensively about his death, her story, and her guilt. It was also around that time in 2012, when I read *Heaven is for Real* and Greg made himself known to me through that first *epiphany* on the plane.

During the astrology reading, Heather also stated that I had the *right* to tell my story, and she recommended that I let my imagination flow to *"that other truth,"* giving Greg a *"sense of purpose."* The *"other truth"* was the truth that Greg came back to this earth through my birth. His spirit returned to work with me to help my mother heal, to help me heal, and to help others heal.

As I walked out of that reading, I knew that I was on a mission: A mission to speak the *Truth* about death and dying, the *Truth* about grief, and to hear the *Truth* from those who grieve.

As I gathered more information about my family, my life, and my spirituality, this book became an intricate web of synchronicities. Why it took me until my mid-fifties to really start figuring it out is not totally understood, but I believe that the sixtieth anniversary of Greg's death moved me rapidly down my spiritual path to live consciously within my *Life Purpose.*

In March of 2015, I was on the retreat where I had first spoken of Greg, when I had another reading, this time with a medium and psychic named Vonne. Vonne asked me if my brother, Greg, had Autism. I told her that Greg was just a little baby when he died, so no one would have known if he had Autism or not.

She said she had a sense that Greg had been born with Autism, and that his transition from this life was due to the fact that had he lived, it would have been a very difficult life for Greg and a great burden for my family.

Isn't it interesting that it was several months prior to that reading when I had asked Taylor, the artistic young woman with Autism, to be the artist to create Greg's portrait for this book?

After I had my reading with Vonne, I sat down with Taylor's mom to ask some questions about having a baby with Autism, specifically, *what was the bonding like with a baby later diagnosed with Autism?*

Taylor's mom, Kristi, said that since Taylor was her first child, she really did not notice anything unusual with regard to her bonding with her child. It was only after having another child that she realized her daughter hadn't *connected* with her like her son did as a baby. Her son engaged right away with her, which was a totally different experience than with Taylor.

As Kristi and I talked, answers came to me for some questions I had been struggling with for the past few years. I had difficulty understanding why my mom always said that she "*never got to know*" Greg.

Mom doesn't have much memory of his four months on this earth, and it feels as if she never saw his personality shine through. *Could this be because he was born with Autism? Is that the reason why my mom never "got to know him?" Did he die from a reaction to his immunization because he was susceptible to the serum? Could it be that there is some truth to the linkage between childhood immunizations and Autism?*

I also had an opportunity during the writing of this book, to meet another young woman. I was visiting at her home with her parents who were recipients of some money raised through a cancer benefit that I co-founded.

As we sat around the table talking, the conversation took on a surreal atmosphere and we all felt the presence of "spirit" within the home. As we were talking about a beloved uncle who had died, I could tell that the young woman had strong intuitive gifts. I looked over at her and acknowledged that I sensed she had some important things to share, it was then that she told me she had been diagnosed with various disorders ranging from *Anxiety* to *Attention Deficit Disorder* to *Depression*.

She said she had recently watched a program on *Asperger's Syndrome*, a higher functioning level on the Autism spectrum. She said that all of the signs that were attributed to Asperger's were ones that she has experienced throughout her life. She questions if she is on the Autism spectrum.

Also during the course of writing this book, I was honored to meet with a woman who was looking for a Life Coach. As we chatted, she shared that she is a mom to a six-year-old child with Autism, a child who is developmentally behind his age group by several years, requiring intensive therapy and care by his teachers and caregivers.

As I talked with this woman, she spoke of the grief she experiences by having a child who has significant challenges. *Was this woman placed in front of me to help me understand what challenges my parents may have faced if Greg had lived?*

Vonne had also predicted that I would be doing some work with families impacted by

Autism.

Was it just happenstance that Vonne asked about Greg possibly having Autism, and now I have people coming into my life dealing with the very issues that my parent's could have potentially dealt with back in the 1950's?

Or is it synchronicity?

Did I unknowingly conjure up connections with people dealing with Autism, or was it part of a greater Divine plan?

No one will ever know why Greg died, but if he did indeed have Autism, life would have been extremely challenging for my parents and our family. I imagine that children born with behaviors of what we know today as severe Autism, would have most likely been institutionalized back in the 1950's, carrying with it great sadness, guilt and grief for their parents.

Chapter 31

I AM a *Healing* Scribe

As I mentioned earlier, I shared the book *Heaven is for Real* with my friend Julie. She read it and in turn gave it to her mother, Elaine, because Julie had a sibling who died at birth, and she thought the book might give some comfort to her mom.

I knew I wanted to interview other mothers, so I could hear their stories, and hopefully find a way to help those who continue to grieve, especially those parents who have known no comfort after the death of their children many years ago. I asked Julie if she would approach her mom to see if she was willing to share her story with me, and Elaine said she would be happy to do so.

I met Elaine and Julie recently to hear Elaine's story, a story that began on July 25, 1964.

Elaine was at full-term and began a very rapid labor. By the time she got to the hospital, the baby was ready to be delivered, but the staff was not ready. The nurses wrapped Elaine's legs together with a bath sheet to stop the baby from exiting the womb, because the doctor had not arrived at the hospital yet.

Elaine recalls being *"knocked out"* by the anesthetist while they were waiting for the doctor to come. She said that when they finally gave her permission to push, it only took two pushes, and her baby girl was born as a stillbirth. Up until the time she went into the hospital, Elaine said the baby had been very active and there was no indication of distress.

As Elaine continued with her story, it became a bit disjointed as she tried to get out all of the memories, not wanting to miss any details. She told me that after the baby was born, the nurses quickly moved Elaine to an *isolation* room, saying that she had some type of infection, something I sensed she does not believe to this day.

She recalls her parents coming to see her, but they were unable to come into her room. She remembers her father standing in the doorway, as her eyes looked off into the distance, and she spoke of the gentle man who was moved to anger because of the circumstances surrounding the death of his grandchild.

Elaine believes that her baby girl had inhaled the amniotic fluid and died because she was not able to exit the womb. Fifty years later, one can sense the anger starting to bubble over as she remembers that day so long ago. Another mother, caught in the talons of grief, which have never loosened its grip after all of these years.

When I inquired what her child's name was, Elaine said she was not "*allowed to name the baby*" because her husband wanted to "*save the name*" in case they had another daughter.

As she spoke, more anger bubbled up; anger that her daughter was not recognized by her name, a name that had already been picked out for her. I asked permission to call the baby by her given name, and I could tell that Elaine had been holding the name of her baby in her heart for these many years. *Donna.*

My friend, Julie, had sent me a picture of a stone marker on a gravesite over Memorial weekend last year, it was a picture of a tiny stone bearing the name of *Baby Girl (last name)*. It was the gravesite of the little baby we now know as Donna.

Elaine still grieves, much like my mother, because she was never able to hold her child, or even gaze upon her little face. She only caught a glimpse as the nurses whisked the infant away immediately following her birth.

Elaine then began to describe Donna, even though she hadn't really seen her but for a brief moment. She shared with me that Donna looked like her oldest daughter, and then Elaine looked up at me and said, *"She was going to be a smart child."* It was as if Elaine knew intuitively who her child was even though she had never spent time with her after her birth.

As we talked, Elaine's eyes would fill with tears. Sometimes they were tears of *hurt* that would surface, and then they were gone. The tears would surface again, only as tears of *anger*, and then just as quickly as they came, the tears would recede, once again to come back as tears of *sadness*. Sadness because Donna was taken from her so abruptly.

So many tears and broken dreams.

Elaine recalls that she *"never slept for six weeks"* after Donna died. She could not sleep, and her life was enveloped in a thick fog. Her husband told their other four children to not speak about the baby because it would *upset* their mother. Unfortunately, the reality was that Elaine wanted to speak of this little girl. She wanted to name her little girl. She wanted to grieve.

As a Catholic, Elaine was told that Donna went to "limbo," because that is where the Catholic Church said unbaptized babies went. Being told her baby was not going immediately to Heaven was a belief that Elaine would not agree with, yet I could tell that it created anger within her for years.

Like my mother, the beliefs of the Church created a compounded sadness. Sadness that the Church did not honor their children was layered upon the sadness that their children were no longer of this world.

Elaine also shared that she became pregnant three years after the death of Donna - another child lost - after she suffered a miscarriage when she was a little over six months pregnant. Elaine also had named this little baby boy. Jon was immediately whisked away after his birth, and once again, Elaine was unable to see her child. His mommy was never able to hold him in her arms.

When Jon was taken to the local funeral home, Elaine asked the funeral director what happened to babies that were miscarried. The funeral director told her that they wrapped up those babies and when another person died, they were placed in the grave of that person as a way to allow those babies to be buried at the local cemetery.

Elaine later found out that little Jon was buried with *"Mr. Larson,"* and she told me that knowing her baby was taken care of and *"put to rest"* with another, gave her great comfort.

It was interesting to interview Elaine with her daughter Julie present. Julie was six years old, but says that she does not remember much about that time in her life. When Elaine asked Julie if she remembered her mom laying on the sofa for six weeks in a dark depression, Julie could only shake her head *"no."*

Julie had thought for years, that her baby sister was going to be called Karen. She had never heard her mom talk about wanting to name this little girl, Donna. Here was another family who lay to rest a tiny child, never to be spoken of again.

Grief is deeply personal and very private, yet shared by so many.

As fate would have it, another woman showed up during the course of the writing of this book; another woman whose story needed to be heard.

Karrie is an old friend of mine who I met when I was sixteen, and she was a young *Hippie momma* with what seemed like a full tribe of little kids running or crawling around! She had three little girls and then Mikey came along. Mikey was the wee one, her only boy amidst three older sisters.

I remember how in awe I was of this free-spirited woman who could play a guitar and sing with a voice that easily mirrored the likes of Joan Baez or Carole King. A beautiful, sexy woman who exuded strength that emanated from her very soul. One would never have imagined the challenges and heartbreak she was going to endure over the next forty years.

Karrie and her husband were the couple that played hard and loved hard, and then one day he left and moved to Alaska. I remember being shocked to hear the news that they had split up, and even more shocked when later, we heard that he had taken his own life. This was a devastating loss for the woman who had loved him with her heart and soul and a devastating loss to his four babies.

When Karrie's son Mikey was a young adult, he too, died at his own hand, another tragic death in this family.

Karrie and I had not seen each other in probably thirty years and had only recently reconnected via Facebook a few years ago, so I was not aware of the circumstances surrounding Mikey's death until several months ago, when my husband and I invited her over for dinner.

I didn't have to say a word before Karrie's story began to flow from her. She went into graphic detail of what happened that day so many years ago. She remembers exactly where she was and how she knew immediately when Mikey's life ended, because she physically felt it in her own body. There was no anger in her voice as she shared her story, just an achingly deep sadness as she recalled the worst day of her life.

As with any parent who has had a child die, not one day goes by without her thinking of her child, her child who may not be physically here on Earth, but is definitely with his momma each and every day in spirit. She can feel him. She can sense what he is saying to her. She has the deep abiding *Faith* that his life didn't end with death because his soul continues to live on.

Karrie will be one of the first people to tell you hat her life was far from perfect before Mikey's death. It could have been very easy for Karrie to never surface again once he died. It would have been easy for her to stay deep within the depths of depression for the remainder of her life, but she didn't.

Karrie was like the other mothers who knew that they needed to pull themselves together because they had other children to support and love. She climbed slowly out of the depths of Hell with purpose: Purpose to stop the cycle of depression that ran prevalent in the genetics of her children and purpose to be a loving grandma to the generation after her children.

Karrie is a heroine in my eyes. She walked a very dark and lonely path for many years. Her body is no longer that of the lithe, sexy woman with dark hair down to her waist. She struggles to breathe if an oxygen tank is not close at hand, and yet she still remains that epitome of strength I knew when I was sixteen.

She still remains that beautiful young woman; only there is a different look in her eyes now. The look that I have seen in so many mothers who have lost their child, a look that floats off into the distance, remembering in detail the ones who left them.

Why is Karrie my heroine? Because she has shown me what true *Faith* is all about. *Faith* that this life is not the only one. *Faith* that we will be reunited with our loved ones when we leave this earth. *Faith* that the challenges we endure on this earth can make us stronger, more loving, and a comfort to others, if we allow ourselves to do so.

Prior to writing Karrie's story, I sent her a message on March 8, 2016 to ask her permission to share her story of grief. I told her I wanted to honor Mikey and her in this book, to honor their stories, and to share how holding onto Faith has kept her going day by day. She responded that day saying she would be honored.

The following day, I asked her for a picture of Mikey because I wanted to channel him while I was writing because I love to gaze at the children's photos to see their faces and to feel that connection.

Karrie said that Mikey was a very kind and loving person. She said she always called him her *"old soul, because he just knew so many things beyond his years."*

As I was writing their story, I got an intuitive hit – a message that the depression that haunted his father also haunted Mikey and one of his sisters. I also wondered if that sister, who is a very gifted singer and songwriter, ever felt her brother's spirit with her when she is singing.

I decided to ask Karrie if any of what I was picking up on made sense to her and she responded: *"Mikey transitioned on March 8, 1999. Lizzy, his sister, wrote all of the songs that were on his Facebook page, and yes, she says she feels his presence around her when she sings them."*

Karrie also told me that Mikey had a picture of his dad that was taken in Viet Nam when his dad was nineteen. Karrie said you could not tell the two of them apart, they looked so much alike. When Mikey died, he was wearing his boxers and his dad's class ring, with his dad's picture pinned at eye level. They were both dressed exactly the same way.

I was so emotionally touched by what Karrie had shared, and I felt a strong sense of remorse from both Mikey and her ex-husband for the circumstances of their death. I could see them both in my mind's eye, gazing at her with such pure love and light as they both apologized deeply for the way that they both died.

I sent a message to Karrie explaining all that I had "sensed" from both Mikey and his dad, and then I told her I needed to go take a walk to get "grounded" because it was so emotional, yet I was so honored that they both came through for her.

As I was getting ready to get up from my computer to go for a walk, I felt a push to look at the calendar. It was March 10, 2016, meaning that Mikey's anniversary of his death was just two days prior. How synchronistic that I reached out to Karrie for permission to write her story on the anniversary of Mikey's death, and that I started writing their story at that particular time when I had no clue that was the date of his death.

Coincidence? I think not.

Michael (Mikey) Juergens

❖

There is no greater loss than that of a child. No matter if the child was a baby, a toddler, a teenager, or an adult... it is all the same loss when one is a parent.

Chapter 32

Faith, Hope, and Love

Throughout this journey of hearing the stories of grieving parents, I have found that parents who have found some joy in their lives after the death of their children have one common denominator. It is called **_FAITH_**.

I think my mom lost a bit of her faith when Greg died, and I believe Elaine lost a bit of her faith when Donna was not allowed to come into this world naturally. Cindy shared with me that she did lose her faith when Angie

411

died, and is now wondering how to regain it back and how to trust fully in God again.

Did these women completely lose faith? No, because I know from talking to each one of them that they still believe in Heaven. They all continue to hope and pray that they will be reunited with their children in the next life.

However, I do think that they lost a little bit of faith in some of their Church's teachings and beliefs. I think they lost some faith that God stood beside them during the most awful time of their lives.

As a grieving parent, they have difficulty believing that there may be a greater purpose being served by the deaths of their children. All of these women have lived abundant lives, yet they have not experienced a life filled with an unending sense of *Joy*.

Finding Joy is not dishonoring of your loved ones who have died. It honors them because their soul does not want you to stop living... their spirit means for you to live...their spirit means for you to continue to love...

The parents who appear to be able to move forward and create a great purpose in their lives lean on that spiritual faith, like Karrie, and truly embrace the belief their children are being taken care of in Heaven. They have faith, that the grief is not their burden to carry alone.

These are the parents who volunteer at Grief Camps. These are the parents like Jill Stephenson, who choose to work with soldiers with the hope to make a difference and create purpose from the deaths of their military sons and daughters.

These are the parents also like Jill, who use their stories to educate on how organ donation can save lives, and bring purpose out of the deaths of their children.

These are the parents who stand up on

podiums to tearfully share their stories of the most painful time of their lives, using their tragedy as a platform to educate on suicide, drug and alcohol abuse, or driving while distracted.

These are the parents who bring forth additional children into the world so that they can nurture new lives. These are the parents who retained or regained their **FAITH** through:

Finding Awesome Inspiration To Heal

Chapter 33

The Ho'oponopono

When I went on that spiritual retreat in March of 2015, I learned about **Ho'oponopono** – a Hawaiian *prayer* that gained notoriety after being used by Dr. Hew Len, a psychologist at Hawaii State Hospital, a facility which housed those who were deemed criminally insane.

Under Dr. Hew Len's tenure, the prison environment changed. Inmates improved in their behaviors, shackles were removed, patients were discharged, staff absenteeism decreased and people actually wanted to work at the prison. Ultimately, the ratio of patients to staff became so low because of the successful rehabilitation of the patients (prisoners) that the prison closed down.

The darkness had lifted.

Dr. Len believed that as a human being, he was responsible for everything in his life including all of the patients at that hospital. Being responsible meant that he needed to take some ownership in their healing, and because of that ownership, he was to ask for forgiveness on behalf of all who had inflicted some harm on those prisoners.

When I was doing a little research about Dr. Hew Len, the tune, *"We are the World"* popped into my head:

"We are the world, we are the children. We are the ones who make a brighter day so let's start giving. There's a choice we're making, we're saving our own lives...
When you're down and out, there seems no hope at all but if you just believe, there's no way we can fall..."

I understood what Dr. Len was saying. We are all part of a much bigger family, and when a member of our family is suffering, we can take responsibility to help heal them through healing ourselves. Per Dr. Hew Len, the act of healing is very simple, saying this simple prayer with true conviction:

"I am Sorry.
Forgive Me.
I Love You.
Thank You."

419

I actually had the opportunity to try Dr. Len's philosophy within my family on Father's Day of 2015. Father's Day of that year also fell on Greg's birthday. That morning, I prayed to God, Greg, and all of the Angels to help me take that big, brave step, of asking my mom for forgiveness on behalf of all of those people involved with the hurt surrounding Greg's death.

I wasn't exactly sure how to proceed, and to be perfectly honest; I was scared. My fear was that I might possibly create more pain for my mom, yet I knew that it was an important step for her to maybe find some healing in her grief.

I went to the store on that Father's Day with the intention of buying roses for Greg and Dad's gravesites, but I ended up walking away with many more.

I went home, put three roses in a bud vase, and brought them to my mom. She looked at me with surprise when I tearfully told her that they were from Greg. She thanked me and then gave me a bit of a *look* and told me to not cry as the tears were welling up in my eyes and rolling down my cheeks.

I asked Mom to go with me to the cemetery where our first stop was at her parents' gravesite. It was *intentional* to start at their graves because my mom so loved her father, and I thought it would be nice to spend a few minutes reminiscing and honoring my grandfather with her. My mother spoke of his gentleness, and of his being a man of few words. She said he wasn't outwardly affectionate but she knew her father loved her deeply.

It was at that gravesite, when I asked my

mom if I could do something, to ask forgiveness for all who had hurt her in her life. I knew I needed to do this while standing at my grandmother's grave, because in my mom's mind, my grandmother was a bit removed from much of my mother's life. My mother also does not remember her mother reaching out and consoling her grieving daughter when my brother died.

I once again started crying, as I asked my mom for permission to say a prayer. I could tell my request puzzled her when she stated, *"No one has hurt me!"* I told her that I thought this might be good for her to heal, by allowing me to ask for forgiveness on behalf of those who were not there for her when Greg died, including my grandmother, my dad, or anyone else who may have caused her pain.

My mom granted me permission.

I stood in front of her and as we clasped our hands together across the gravestone of my grandparents, I prayed the Ho'oponono: *"I Love You. I am Sorry. Forgive Me,"* and then my mom interrupted me and said, *"You never did anything to me."* So I explained to her again that I was doing this on behalf of those who could not speak. I then finished the prayer with, *"Thank You."*

My mom looked up at me and said softly, *"I accept."*

Just that.

We then walked quietly to the car, and I drove her a little further down the cemetery road, telling her that there was another person I thought she should give a rose to. She again looked a little puzzled as I pulled up and gently guided her to Ben's gravestone, her long lost love that she was engaged to long before she met my dad.

Mom looked a bit surprised but willingly walked with me to Ben's headstone and placed the rose on it's ledge as I cleared away the dead grass. She voiced that she was happy that he had had a home all those years, with people who could take care of him after his mental illness took over his life.

We then walked the short way over to Greg and Dad's gravestones. I placed a rose on Dad's grave for Father's Day and mom placed a rose on Greg's grave. I added two more roses to Greg's grave and together, mom and I remembered him, remembered his short life, and acknowledged his spirit.

Mom looked at me as we walked away and said that after Greg died, she just wanted to come out to the cemetery and *"dig him up,"* so she could bring him home with her. I gently gave her a hug and told her that was a very normal reaction – I can tell you that hearing my little elderly momma speak of wanting to dig up the dirt with her bare hands to hold her tiny child nearly broke my heart.

The act of burying a child definitely has to be the greatest heartache of all.

Later that evening, as I was getting ready to go on a work trip the following morning, I decided to open up some birthday cards that were on the counter that were left for me by my family - it was my birthday the next day.

I opened the card from my mom and she had a little notecard with a message written in her frail, tiny handwriting: *"I thank Harold (my dad) and God for giving me a daughter."* I immediately began to cry because this was the first time in my life that my mom was able to say something about my dad with love. The power of that simple prayer of forgiveness had done its magic. My mom finally experienced some healing from so long ago.

My purpose for writing this book was to create some healing for my mom and to let her know that Greg and I honor her, and that day at the cemetery brought it all to fruition. The journey that began in November of 2014 after the family grief camp had completed its course on June 21st, 2015.

My hope is that my mom can transition with peace in her heart and soul when the time comes for her to leave this earth. I know she will be welcomed into the loving arms of my dad, her ex-fiance Ben, my grandparents, her friends, and most of all she will be able to see through her eyes the light of Greg's spirit. She will be able to hold the soul of her child in her arms once again.

This story is ending but its message is not. Grief knows no boundaries and has no shelf life. It can affect anyone, anywhere, and at any time. Losinga child is losing a piece of oneself. The heart of the parent explodes with tremendous force, shattering their world into a million pieces.

This story is also about the children who remain (or are born after) a sibling who dies. My hope is that anyone who reads this book who knows of a family with child loss, will reach out and help the whole family by connecting with the children in addition to the parents. To bring some thread of hope to help mend the torn fabric of the family.

I believe Greg needed to leave this world in orderto be a healing light. In 1952, Greg was born, and then he died. He died in order to be reborn. He was reborn through my life, my mother's memories, and through this book, so that he could be *The Mourning's Light*.

I feel that it is appropriate to end this story by sharing a Facebook post that was posted last year by Caycie Volek (with her permission).

"Thought I'd share the best advice my Mom has ever given me. When my sister was 7 she was killed in an accident. My uncle was getting married a month later and my Mom had bought us three girls all new dresses for the special day. Angie asked to wear her new dress all the time and Mom always said no. Well Angie died before the wedding and was buried in the dress... I had my own little girl who wanted to wear her Easter

dress to the grocery store and my Mom said 'life is to short to not wear the dress, let her wear the dam(sp) Dress.' I live every day by that motto. Life is too short to not dance in the rain, or eat the cookie or wear rain boots and a tutu with a superman cape to Target ☺"

If you know of anyone who has suffered through the loss of a child, I hope you will walk away with a few lessons from this book:

❖ Allow the parents and the siblings to tell their stories (even if you are hearing them for the hundredth time).

❖ Honor the child who died by saying his/her name.

❖ Follow the family's lead: When they want to talk – talk. When they want to sit in silence – sit in silence.

❖ Love them unconditionally.

Pat and her Momma (Ruth age 91)

ACKNOWLEDGEMENTS

I want to thank all who have helped me bring this book to fruition. A very special thanks to *Children's Grief Connection* for allowing me into their family.

A tremendous amount of gratitude is extended to the Burpo family in sharing Colton's story for the world to read.

A heartfelt thank you to all of the grieving moms and siblings for sharing their stories with me including: Jill Stephenson, Julie Dahl and her mother Elaine, Karrie Kemp, Cindy

Corbit and her daughter Caycie, and Keith Krueger and those mothers and daughters who have shared their stories but remain anonymous to honor their personal and private stories.

A huge thank you to my AwEsOmE (as Molly F. would write it) spiritual teachers including: Molly Friedenfeld, Jill Sand, Laurie Wondra, and Vonne Jonnsen.

I bow in thanks to my artistic friends: Wendy Hurd Creative LLC and Taylor Zappa. Thank you also to Taylor's mom Kristi, for helping me understand what it is like having a newborn with Autism.

Thank you to my beta-readers: Betsy Brown Theis and Jeffrey Forthun. Also a huge bouquet of gratitude to Jill Sand and Betsy Brown Theis for their gift of editing.

To my children: Tommy and Caitlin, thank you for giving us two incredible grand-daughters who have taught me to love with total abandon. Having grandchildren is the best form of mind-body therapy that anyone could ever have!

To my daughter Brittany, thank you for being my Virtual Assistant and being there when the first epiphany struck – who would have imagined that day that I exited the plane would have turned into a book!

To my son Trevor, thank you for holding down the fort and tolerating my "whooey-ness" these past few years! You are the inspiration for me to take the plunge and write a book!

To my husband Ken, what can I say that would ever be adequate in form of a thank you? You always have my back, you believe in me, and you love me without fail. I thank God, the Universe, and our little souls of the Sun who made our contract come to fruition. I love you to infinity and beyond!

To my mother, Ruth Huss, my gratitude and love overflow to you for giving Greg life, for giving me life, for being the best mom you could, and teaching me that a mother's love for her child will never die.

I LOVE YOU

Bibliography and Resources

Burpo, Todd with Vincent, Lynn; *Heaven Is for Real (2010, 2011)* Thomas Nelson, Inc. Nashville, Tennessee

Walsch, Neale Donald; *The Little Soul and the Sun (1998)* Hampton Roads Publishing Company, Inc. Charlottesvill, VA 22902

For more information on the Ho'oponopono and Dr. Ihaleakala Hew Len Ph.D.,:
www.zero-wise.com

For more information about Jill Stephenson, Motivational Speaker for organ donation advocacy:

www.iamjillstephenson.com

For more information on Children's Grief Connection and Hearts of Hope Camps:

www.childrensgriefconnection.com

For more information on The Compassionate Friends organization:

www.compassionatefriends.org

For more information on SAVE – Suicide prevention information, suicide, depression awareness:

www.save.org

For more information and resources regarding Autism Spectrum Disorder:

www.autismspeaks.org

Patricia (Pat) Sheveland

ABOUT THE AUTHOR

Patricia (Pat) Sheveland, RN, CMC, PCC, Founder of Positive Aspects Today, LLC, is a certified life coach through the International Coaching Federation (ICF).

As a child born into a grieving family, Pat's mission in life is to be a *light for those who mourn*.

As an intuitive light coach, a mind-body-spirit health practitioner, and a motivational speaker, her life is dedicated to helping people find some healing from grief by creating lives filled with *Purpose* and *Joy*.

Pat is a *recovering* corporate executive, retiring from her twenty-five year corporate career in early 2016 to pursue her dream of working (aka playing) in her coaching practice on a full time basis.

When she is not coaching, writing, sharing her story, or facilitating group coaching events, Pat loves to spend her time riding her Harley Tri-Glide and going *up north* to their river home in Central Minnesota.

Pat lives in Shakopee, Minnesota with her husband, her mom, and their two standard size Labradoodles (Gus and Gracee).

To learn more about Pat, her services and events, please visit her website

at

www.patsheveland.com

You can also contact Pat via her website to schedule private coaching sessions, speaking engagements, retreats or group healing events.

Made in United States
Orlando, FL
05 June 2023

33858708R00268